The Handbook for Touring Bicyclists

Frosty Wooldridge

Chockstone Press
Evergreen, Colorado

To my mother Vivien, my father Howard, my brothers Rex, Howard, John, and sister Linda. My dear friends.

Cover Photo: Gary Hall
Illustrations: Scott Annis

ISBN: 1-57540-024-3

Published and Distributed by
Chockstone Press, Inc.
Post Office Box 3505
Evergreen, Colorado 80439

Contents

Thanks

Few people do anything alone with much success. It has been my privilege to work with the Chockstone Press staff. Their consummate professionalism and first class excitement made writing this book a pleasure.

My dear thanks goes to the following friends who critiqued the original manuscript and added to its final excellence. Thank you: Gary Hall, Doug Armstrong, Bryan Deley, Sandi Lynn, Kevin Riggs, Judy Bennett, Scott Creevy, Howard Wooldridge, Al Hymer, Debbie Chenoweth, John Conrad, Paul Austin, John Brown, Pam Howell, Nancy Steller, Marti Yarington, Pam Cerveny.

Thanks for the miles of smiles everyone of you.

Prologue to Being on Tour

"Bicycle adventure means you're pedaling into mysterious regions with a sense of high expectation. You pedal toward the unknown because you may see something beyond your imagination. That's what brought you there."

The Gourmet Bicyclist

Onward

Bicycle touring creates "goose bump" moments of adventure rarely understood by the American vacationing public. Many travelers in automobiles see heavily loaded bicycles and say to themselves, "Those people are crazy...I'm glad it's not me." They see bicycle touring as hard work. What they fail to realize is that men and women on bicycle tours "become" the adventure. Instead of seeing the scenery, cyclists coalesce with it – mentally, physically and spiritually. Their pleasure is manifested by pedaling and eating. Motorists tediously pump fuel into their gas tanks, while bicyclists celebrate – beyond belief – the refueling their bodies.

While pedaling, we become ravenous. No matter how much we stuff our mouths, food is on our minds while we're pedaling down the highway.

Bicyclists gobble trail mix as fast as a tornado devours a chunk of prairie. Bananas are a soft piece of heaven to our palettes. A juicy peach slides over our taste buds with sweet energy as we talk to village locals. An orange puts a smile on a face even as the sun goes down.

On tour, we not only taste food in a new way – we smell it, and feel its texture more intimately. Eating is the source of our power.

Food is fundamental. You absorb it to fire your furnace. It powers you into an adventure, into those peak moments that raise goose bumps on your spirit. Food not only generates energy, it repairs your tissue and muscles. It's the fuel that allows you to pedal your bike. The higher the octane of the food, the more efficient and plentiful the energy output.

Food is fabulous. You, as a touring cyclist, enjoy many types and textures of food. Your raging appetite makes every scent and taste a sensory pleasure.

Food is always on your mind as you roll down the road. Where is the next store? "I'm going to buy a candy bar, or three, and a bag of chips...I should treat myself to a pint, no, a gallon of ice cream...And then some chocolate chip cookies... Hey, there's an all-you-can-eat salad bar..."

Food is fun. For touring cyclists, it's a rest stop that finds you talking with strangers in a small town. You'll hear some humorous stories. A shop keeper might tell you a hilarious tale about the day a skunk ran through her store. Or, after leaning your bike against a tree in some mountainous wilderness, you grab the trail mix, cookies, apples and water bottles. You might make a peanut butter and jam sandwich using your rear pack as a table. You are in the dining room of some mountain mansion. As you stand there, a herd of elk walks past.

At campsites with the cook stove being assembled, I've heard other cyclists exclaim, "Now, let the real adventure begin...F-O-O-D."

On the following pages, you'll discover how to buy, carry, prepare and store food while on tour. Whether you enjoy meat-based meals, or are a vegetarian, you have in your hands exciting recipes for fueling your body.

Bicycle touring is growing in popularity each year. Men and women around the world are taking to the highways and the "open air" is their kitchen.

Are you planning an international tour into Third World countries? You can eat and drink safely with the concepts explained in this book. Are you camping in grizzly country? Learn how to avoid becoming a gourmet meal for the big bears! Will you be cooking at 10,000 feet in the Andes? Find out how. Are you new to bicycle touring? Discover the 'ins and outs' with a "Baker's Dozen." of touring tips that are essential for successful bicycle adventuring. Is romance on your mind? Find out what it means in "Romantic Modifications To Your Candle Lantern."

Whether you're going on a weekend ride, a week-long tour, or two years around the world, this handbook will help you learn the artistry of bicycling and cooking.

Part One
Touring Tips

Recipes for Adventure Destinations

I got home last night – cold, hungry, and tired. I didn't know what to make for dinner. Should I go out for a pizza or cook a meal? I'm so frazzled, I don't know what I want. Maybe I should call up my friend Karen for a few ideas...maybe she could help me decide...Ring, ring...

"You just ate at Rocky's Cantina and they serve fantastic Mexican food?" I asked.

"Yes, they deliver...it's great." she said.

"Okay, what's their number? It's just what I need. Thanks."

The Gourmet Bicyclist

Let's face it, we live in a high speed, fast-paced society. Everyone rushes from work to meetings to home to school to the supermarket to sports events – and back home again to fall into bed – only to get up and do it again the next day. Everything is rush, rush, rush. Weekends fly by so fast! We don't have a chance to relax because we're so busy running around doing errands, trying to catch up. In so many ways, we live our lives like a pack of dogs chasing their tails.

Instead of having more leisure time, we have less. Meals are prepared out of boxes and bags. Was there life before the microwave oven was invented? How did they live back in those Stone-Age days? Vacations are our salvation. For a week or two during the year,we can get off the treadmill and settle into a slower pace. One pace is the easy pleasure of a bicycle tour. It'll get us back into our natural rhythms – refreshing us physically and spiritually.

Where is a good place for touring? We might be out of shape, so we're not looking for the Rocky Mountains. We live in Seattle, meaning we're looking for a desert tour. The kids haven't seen Yellowstone, but is summer a good time of year for a tour there? Maybe we need a support van, just in case.

You have many choices these days, but you want to make intelligent decisions. That means you need to be realistic. Some folks may have a limited budget while others have deep pockets.

If you want a no-hassle guided tour, where your food and sleeping arrangements are prepared in advance, try a tour organized by any of the bicycle tour companies in the back of this book. Backroads and All Adventure Travel will hook you up with the tours around the world. They can customize a tour to your needs. For the most part, they can help you ride in the sunshine. I recommend riding in the sunshine. It brightens your spirit as well as your attitude. Rain-drenched touring experiences make less than desirable bicycling memories. The pictures turn out lousy, too!

You may want to go on a self-guided tour. Depending on the time you have, you need to figure in transport to and from your intended touring area. Make sure you're ready to ride. Take a few weekend tours to complete a "shakedown" of your bike and gear. It's good to have a feeling for what you're doing before you go on a real tour.

On any tour, I recommend you ride around 40 to 50 miles per day if you intend to relax and see the sights. Check for campground locations along your intended route if you're not comfortable with camping in the wild. Check with one of the many auto clubs across the country and pick up a road map that you can use to plan your trip. These maps have a wealth of information on them, including campgrounds.

I have a put together a number of tours that may satisfy your need for something "good" even if you're planning on touring at the last minute. They are listed below. In some cases, I've recommended routes specifically; in others, I've just pointed you in the right direction. The details are left to you.

For short tours, I look for routes with low traffic flow, good roads and peaceful vistas. On most road maps, red, blue and gray roads (colors used to denote the type of road, ie.e four-lane, two-lane, gravel, etc.) offer the best touring, with blue and gray the best. Seeing lakes, rivers and oceans are high on my agenda. Bodies of water bring about a spiritual peace that is magically and serenely seductive to your soul. Mountains, of course, offer boldness and power.

I have personally ridden these tours and have enjoyed them immensely.

One- To Two-Week Tours

Arizona: Tour the Grand Canyon, then backpack down into it. You may want to ride on old Arizona Route 66 for nostalgia's sake. It's quite beautiful.

Arkansas: Ride on Arkansas Route 7 from Harrison in the north, through Dogpatch,USA, and on to Hot Springs National Park. It's a great ride, with many historical stops along the way. Watch out for Booger Hollow! This is a winding river route most of the way with lots of beauty. They say lots of moonshine can be bought in "them thar hills."

California: Ride from San Francisco to Yosemite National Park, and on to Mariposa Grove. Cycling in two mountain ranges make this a gut-buster. When you get to Yosemite, you'll be in heaven. Do it in May or September to avoid the hoards of tourists. The ride over Badger Pass, at 6,000 feet, will lead you to the beauty of the giant trees of Mariposa Grove. Incredible.

California: This one's for desert rats. Ride through Joshua Tree National Monument to Death Valley. You'll see indescribable sunsets and desert beauty. Ride in March and April or October and November to save yourself from the deadly heat. Springtime features a multitude of desert blooms.

Colorado: For those with chiseled thighs. Do the loop from Frisco to Leadville to Twin Lakes, stay two days, then head back to Leadville and Frisco. You will ride over four 11,000-foot-plus passes and see mountains of remarkable beauty. Camp on rivers. You can sample the fantastic history of mining in Leadville and find romance in Frisco on Lake Dillon, with its boats, sailing and camping. You must be in shape.

Colorado: Ride from Boulder to the Maroon Bells. This has been my secret up until now. This is a wonderful ride of 280 miles over four passes. Ride from Boulder to Nederland to Rollinsville and take the dirt road west along the river up over Corona Pass on the old Moffat Railroad route. Descend into Winter Park. From there, go less than a quarter-mile north of Fraser on U.S. Highway 40 to Grand County Road 50, which will take you through old-growth forests on a dirt road. You'll ride along rivers, and see bears, mountain lions, eagles and hawks. Continue up over Ute Pass and down to Colorado Route 9 on the Blue River. Ride into Frisco, then to Leadville and Twin Lakes. Climb up and over Independence Pass into Aspen and complete the route at the Maroon Bells. A great ride! Very, very interesting. I lead tours on this one. Call me for reservations.

Georgia/Virginia: Ride from north Georgia to Front Royal, Virginia along the Blue Ridge Skyline Drive. This is one of the most fun and thrilling rides on a high mountain ridge you can take in the United States. It's got history, old mill houses and romance along every mile of the road. Plus, there are no commercial vehicles! Take two weeks in May or September to miss the crowds.

Idaho: Out of Coeur d'Alene, head south onto Idaho Route 3 and meet with U.S. Highway 95 heading south to Boise. Located among rivers, wildness and peace, this is a serene trip with mega-beauty.

Iowa: For a kick, you might want to join the insanity of the Ragbrai, a bike trip across the state that is held every summer. You'll meet lots of wild and wacky people. Write the tourist bureau of Iowa for information.

Maine: Ride from Brunswick to Bar Harbor, and further up the coast. This is absolutely a ride for lovers. Camden Harbor and Bar Harbor are two of the most romantic places on earth. Tall ships and fishing nets await you. Mt. Desert Island and Arcadia National Park provide extraordinary beauty for cyclists. The best season is midsummer.

Michigan: Ride from Benton Harbor north to the Mackinac Bridge. This ride along Lake Michigan in early summer or early fall is one of incredible color. Either the spring tulips and festivals in Holland, or a blazing riot of colorful leaves in the fall, make this tour exceptional. Michigan folks love cyclists.

Michigan: Pedal from Whitefish Point, along the southern coast of Lake Superior, to Bar Harbor. For those who want to ride in wilderness peace and see lots of moose, ducks, geese, fox, deer, hummingbirds, wild turkey, pheasants and the like, this is a fabulous tour. You'll ride next to the blue waters of Lake Superior and enjoy yourself in the quiet woods of northern Michigan. There is some dirt road riding, but it is well worth it. The colors are stupendous in late September.

Minnesota: Ride from International Falls to Warroad. The route is scenic, pristine and quiet. Bring your mosquito repellent and camera, and enjoy the nice people. Take your mate on a canoe trip along the way. If you ride in the winter, be prepared to freeze your pedals off in the 50 -degree-below-zero temperatures!

Montana/Canada: Ride from Kalispell, Montana to Mt. Robson in British Columbia. There is nothing quite like riding on Waterton-Glacier National Park's Going to the Sun Road, and then through Kootenay, Banff and Jasper National Parks in Canada. This tour will supersede anything imagined. Try to take two weeks to enjoy it all. You'll see grizzlies, moose, mountain sheep, deer and a plethora of wildlife and birds. Dazzling beauty.

Newfoundland: This is a quaint ride through history and a more peaceful way of life. Follow the coast to be near whales and bird life and icebergs. You'll see where Marconi started his radio transmissions. The houses are full of flower boxes and the ocean is your companion.

New Mexico: Ride across the state on U.S. Highway 60 from the western border to Roswell. You can see where Billy the Kid was shot dead in Lincoln, and where they breed race horses at high altitude. Be ready to climb BIG hills!

New York: Ride from Utica on New York Route 28 through the Adirondacks to Glens Falls. This is a roller coaster ride with trees and lakes and old-town friendliness. Lots of farms and fresh produce.

Nova Scotia: Be prepared for rain on these uncommonly beautiful coast rides. Several loops are possible, and old churches abound. Try racing the 50-foot high tides into shore on foot! It's incredibly peaceful. July and August are best bets for sunshine. You can get lost on the many little backroads and meet people who enjoy a slower pace of life.

Oregon: This state was made for touring riders. They even make bike paths for us by charging a half-percent gas tax. Ride from Klamath Falls on Oregon Route 97 up to Bend and head north on state routes 126, 26 and 7 into Hell's Canyon.

Vermont: The New England states in autumn make for exquisite touring. You might try starting in Montpelier and head north to Craftsbury Common, or tour the loop through Greensboro.

Washington: Start from Sedro Woolley in the west and head east on Washington Route 20 to Omak, then head south on state highway 155 toward Elmer City. This is another peaceful ride through mountains and valleys and rivers and wilderness.

Wyoming: Ride from Jackson Hole through Grand Teton National Park to the north side of Yellowstone National Park. You'll encounter mind-bending beauty and see wildlife that's out of this world. You can't take it in without feeling a sense of wonder with every mile. Do it in late May, before the hoards of tourists arrive, or early September, after they leave.

Rides of Several Months

If you have the time, take a long tour to broaden your experiences. There's a whole new world out there on the Gringo Trail.

Seattle, WA to Anchorage, AK: Ride up the Fraser Valley to the Alaska Highway, from Dawson Creek to Anchorage. The trip will take all summer, and is one of the greatest rides, if not the greatest, ride in North America. You'll the Cassiar Highway and meet up with the Alaska Highway. You have to go west on Provincial Route 16 out of Prince George, B.C., and then turn north at Kitwanga on Provincial Route 37, the Cassiar. It meets up with the Alaska Highway at Watson Lake. By all means, at Meziadian Junction, take a ride west through the Valley of the Glaciers into Hyder, Alaska. You can get Hyderized! Tack a dollar bill with your name on it on to the wall with the rest of the $40,000 from other tourists. Mine's above the door as you come into the Alaska Inn! A ride of a lifetime and beyond.

Border to Border – The West Coast Ride: Ride from Vancouver,B.C. to Tijuana, Mexico. More fun than you can shake a stick at. Dip into Yosemite Valley. See the redwoods, whales, porpoises,otters, seals, Golden Gate, Big Sur and much, much more.

Border to Border – The Cascades Route: Ride through the middles of Washington, Oregon and California. You'll be in the mountains all the way. Great ride, great time. The 49er Trail and the Tuba River Valley are outstanding.

Border to Border – The Rocky Mountain Route: Ride from El Paso, Texas north to Calgary, Canada following the Continental Divide. This is an incredible tour. You'll be in the mountains most of the way. You will feel like you've got two coiled springs inside your legs. More than 2,500 miles and tons of fun.

Coast to Coast: Pick a spot anywhere on the West Coast, either Los Angeles, San Francisco, Seattle or Vancouver. Point your bike east and ride to Bar Harbor, Maine, or any place along the East Coast. Invite me to your slide show! What a ride! What a time!

Foreign Tours

New Zealand: Without a doubt, this is a tour where you can't pedal slowly enough. Ride the North and South Islands. Tour from Auckland to Wellington through Rotorura. Take the ferry to Pictin and then ride the east coast to Invercargill. Ride up the west coast through the Franz-Josef Glacier and end up back in Pictin. Take this ride after mid-February or you will find the the definition of "dry" in the Kiwi dictionary under the word "miracle." This is one of the most peaceful, bucolic, pastoral, serene and beautiful rides in the world. More than twenty-one million sheep await you. Take the Milford Trek, see Milford Sound, see the Miroki Boulders, the penguins, seals, birds, mountains and much more. It's fantastic.

Australia: Ride in Tasmania. It's fabulous. Then, for another astounding tour, ride the Great Ocean Road from Melbourne to Adelaide.

Japan: Riding in Japan is an extraordinary experience. The Japanese will love you and treat you with honor. The mountains and seaside are beautiful.

China: If you do nothing else in your life, ride to the Great Wall Of China. China is a great big place with a fascinating culture, and there are many tours and scenic routes. See Beijing, the Summer Palace, the tombs of the Ming Dynasty and the Forbidden City. Try to ride a junk on the Yangtze River in Shanghai.

Norway: Ride from the south of the country to the north, and cross the Arctic Circle. You'll see fjords and oceans and quiet towns. My brother lives in Radol – stop in for a visit. He and his wife Kari love international visitors. Look in the phone book for his name.

Europe: You can't miss wherever you tour in Europe. The history and ambience is simply beautiful.

Greece: You won't be able to get enough of the statues and the Parthenon and the azure waters along the Mediterranean coast.

South America: Perhaps the greatest week-long ride of my life was from La Paz, Bolivia to Arica, Chile. The El Camino Highway, all dirt and no bridges, climbed from 12,500 feet to nearly 16,000 feet and dropped back to sea level. We portage dozens of rivers and had to strip the bikes and carry the gear across on our shoulders. It was an unbelievable ride! If you're not used to high altitude, start in Arica on the coast and head toward La Paz, Bolivia. When you reach La Paz, you can ski at 17,688 feet on the highest ski resort in the world. Magnificent beauty.

That's it for quick tour recipes. You would need several lifetimes to ride in the many places this planet has to offer. Each rider has his or her favorite routes. While you're on the road, listen to the suggestions of other riders and incorporate them into your future plans.

As Bilbo Baggins said in *The Hobbit:* "There's a whole world of adventure waiting just outside your door."

What To Take And Where To Pack It

"Preparation is nine tenths of success."

**The Gourmet Bicyclist,
crying big alligator tears along a lonely highway in Texas
in 104 degrees heat
with a blown tube and no patches in his pack, 1984**

One of the most frustrating feelings for a bicycling tourist is when he digs into his pack for something and can't find it. Even worse is realizing he didn't bring it. It can be as small as a pair of tweezers or as important as a spoke wrench. The best way to prevent such a calamity is to keep a pack list that you can check off before leaving for your adventure.

Special precautions must be taken in ten areas each time you load your gear into your panniers. When you need an item, you want it easily available. That goes double for your first aid kit.

International touring requires extra attention to details, and at least three months of advance preparation.

Equipment Organization

Organizing your equipment is the best way to have it ready for your use. When your gear is packed, especially on your first trip, it may take a few days of rearranging everything to place it where you like it. You'll develop your own preferences. Once that's accomplished, draw a schematic of where everything is placed. Use it for quick reference when packing for future rides.

If it's small, light and you use it often, the best storage place is a zipper pouch on the left rear pannier. Depending on how you stand your bike, items used often need to be on the free side of the bicycle. For efficiency, group similar items like a tooth brush and soap in the same nylon "ditty" bag. These drawstring pouches are handy. You can use clear plastic bags to separate clothes into organized compartments. You can do the same for tire repair tools.

Weight Distribution

The first rule in bicycle touring is: if you don't need or use it, leave it. Why? Simple – weight adds up quickly. Every excess pound you pack will cost you in bike stability and miles covered daily.

When loading your bicycle, you need to balance weight from side to side. More weight should be in the rear panniers than in the front. If you experience a shimmy in your handlebars, it means you have too much in your handlebar bag. Keep less than four pounds in it. If a shimmy persists, lighten your front panniers and check the side to side balance. Traditional touring bikes with light frames and skinny tires have more of a shimmy problem than mountain bikes converted to touring. That's why I recommend a mountain bike.

When riding with four panniers, you need to pack the heaviest equipment – like the stove, frying pan and cable lock – into the lowest sections of your rear panniers. That will keep your "lean" weight – the amount of weight you have on the bike and where it is located – closer to the ground. If you pack heavy items higher up in the panniers, the bike will be top heavy.

The Big Items

Your tent, sleeping bag, day pack and air mattress are bulky pieces that must be balanced over the rear axle. Strap your tent forward under the seat and your tent behind it. The air mattress will fit over the tent. A second set of crossed bungee cords will secure your day pack on top. If you have a front rack, strap your sleeping bag to the top of it. Otherwise, you will have to attach it to your rear rack. Check for hanging straps or bungee cords every time you finish packing your bicycle. Otherwise, you will wrap them around the freewheel or spokes. The result scan tear up your wheel alignment and worse.

Fuel Bottle Placement

You will find your own style for placing equipment. However, the fuel bottle is a potentially troublesome item. Some riders place it in their lower water bottle clip on the down tube. You can wrap it in plastic and set it upright in the rear pouch of your pannier. In either case, be certain to secure the opening from leakage.

Camera Equipment Care

Keep your camera equipment in plastic bags at all times. While on tour, dust swirls around you from cars and the wind. Also, you must be concerned about rain. Large freezer bags work well, and you can see through them and reuse them. Keep camera gear in a day pack cushioned over your air mattress roll on the rear panniers.

Day Pack

A 1,600- to 2,200-cubic-inch internal frame pack with three side compartments is an excellent addition to your versatility while on tour. You can store the camera in it, along with extra film, valuables and food. Make it the easy-access pack holding your most-often used gear. When stopping at a restaurant, or whenever leaving the bike unattended for a few moments, you can release the bungee stretch cords that attach it to your panniers and sling the pack over your shoulders.

Rain-Proofing Your Gear

No doubt about it, you're at the mercy of the elements on a bicycle tour. Your equipment must be kept dry. Wrap everything each morning in plastic bags. Keep your rain gear available. Make certain your film and camera gear is rain-proof. Do the same for your sleeping bag and tent.

Night Light In Your Tent

You have two options in a candle lantern, which is an excellent night light. One is an oil-burning lamp and the other is a nine-hour wax candle – both encased in a lantern. Either costs about $20 and will give you ample light for writing or cooking dinner. I prefer the candles because I can replace them in most countries. If you choose the oil burning lantern, be prepared to have it spill inside your pack. Murphy's Law will stalk you at every turn. Please note: A burning candle lantern in a tent is a dangerous item. Never ever leave it unattended.

Cycling Shoes, Gloves, Glasses, Shorts And Helmet

Buy the best, most comfortable cycling shoes you can afford. Do not ride with tennis shoes. You need the plastic or steel shank on the bottom of the shoe to give you protection from the pedals. Without that shank, you will be in a lot of pain and will waste a lot of energy to compensate.

Buy a good pair of cycling gloves to protect you from pounding your hands to death. The first week of a cycling trip, shake your hands at regular intervals so you won't crush the ulnar nerve in the palm of your hand. It will stay numb for a long time if you don't relieve it by shaking out your hands.

With the ozone vanishing, you need to buy 100% UV-protective sunglasses to prevent damage to your eyes. They should have maximum sun blockage, leather side flaps to protect you from the wind and a cord to keep them around your neck.

Buy two pairs of cycling shorts, either Lycra or baggy touring shorts. Make sure you buy the suede-padded shorts instead of leather, because suede is easier to wash and wear. If you are riding in extremely sunny weather, you might want to wear thin wicking (Thermax) protection in the form of a shirt that covers your arms and neck. If it's blistering sunshine, I recommend you wear thin tights to protect your legs as well. Your body does not need all that sun. You risk skin cancer and worse. Protect your face daily with maximum sun block.

Always wear a helmet. The most serious head injuries occur because riders weren't wearing helmets. Be certain to have a visor on your helmet for sun protection.

Packing List

This packing list below includes many items that are optional. You won't need an extra rear derailleur while pedaling across the United States, but in China, you may need one. Pick what you need for your particular adventure.

If you do not have panniers with the following side pockets, you may have to place your spare items from top to bottom in your panniers in order of use while on tour. If it's not used often, it can go to the bottom of the pannier. Work out a system and customize it for your needs.

Handlebar Bag

1. Map
2. Sunblock lotion
3. Lip balm
4. Post cards/stamps
5. Two pens
6. Sunglasses
7. Schematic of gear location
8. Insect repellent
9. Wallet, money, credit cards
10. Travel book, points of interest
11. Hostel card and handbook
12. Extra passport pictures for visas
13. Riding gloves
14. Scuba diving card
15. International driver's license
16. Dog repellent
17. Compass
18. Bird book if you're a bird watcher
19. Swiss Army Knife
20. Neck bandanna

Left Rear Pannier

Main Compartment

1. Cook stove
2. Fuel bottle
3. Mess kit
4. Fork, spoon, potato peeler, spatula
5. Can opener
6. Matches or lighter (matches in a film canister to waterproof)
7. Frisbee (optional)
8. Tablecloth
9. Extra plastic bottles, spice bottles
10. Butane cartridges
11. Water filter

Lower Left Rear Outside Pouch

1. First aid kit and book
2. Snake bite kit
3. Folding one-gallon water container
4. Thirty feet of nylon cord
5. Athletic tape
6. Knee wrap
7. Butterfly closure suture
8. Band aids
9. Suture line and needle
10. Sewing kit
11. Water purification tablets

Upper Left Rear Outside Pouch

1. Flashlight
2. Spare brake and gear cable
3. Spare brake pads
4. Spare pulleys

Rear Outside Pouch

1. Extra film
2. Used film
3. Night light and strap
4. Spare toe clip and strap
5. Copies of passport, birth certificate, driver's license

Right Rear Pannier

Main Compartment

1. Walking pants
2. Wool mittens
3. Stocking cap

4. One pair wool socks
5. Two pairs of cotton or polypropylene socks
6. Two pairs of underpants
7. Extra polypropylene or Thermax jersey
8. Two pairs of riding shorts
9. Dress clothes (polo shirt, nice pants)
10. Wool sweater
11. Wool, polypropylene or Thermax tights
12. Spare spokes with nipples (four front, six rear)
13. Waterproof/breathable jacket or nylon rainproof jacket
14. Hostel sheet
15. Neoprene warm booties
16. Reading glasses
17. Two half-gallon or 1 one-gallon collapsible water containers

For women:

1. Bras
2. Tampons/panty liners
3. Leg warmers
4. Blouse/skirt
5. Rain booties
6. Bathing suit
7. Cosmetics
8. Hair dryer (Yes, my girl brings hers for dancing nights!)
9. Petroleum jelly
10. Moisturizer

Lower outside pouch

1. Tool kit:
   a. open wrenches, 4 to 12 mm
   b. Allen wrenches, all sizes to fit bike
   c. spoke wrench
   d. spare nuts and bolts (assorted)
   e. wire
   f. pliers
   h. multi-head screwdriver
   i. six-inch crescent wrench
   j. chain breaker
   k. freewheel cog remover
   l. spare chain
   m. spare ball bearings
   n. bottom bracket puller
2. Chain spray
3. Grease cloth

4. Frame-mounted air pump
5. Extra rear derailleur (international tour)
6. Spare freewheel (international tour)
7. Pocket vice
8. Crank remover
9. Ball bearing grease
10. Nylon foot warmers
11. Candle lantern, spare candles
12. Seam sealer (extra tube)
13. Crazy glue
14. Fifty feet of black parachute cord
15. Air pump

Upper Outside Pouch
1. Two spare tubes
2. Two tire patch kits
3. Air gauge
4. Valve stem remover
5. Toilet paper
6. Camera tripod

Front Right Pannier
Main Compartment (With Food Stores)
1. Travel kit:
   a. fingernail clippers
   b. biodegradable soap
   c. tweezers
   d. shaver
   e. toothbrush
   f. toothpaste
   g. dental floss
   h. shampoo
   i. deodorant
   j. cotton swabs
   k. antifungal ointment
   l. cortizone cream (Micatin)
   m. diarrhea medicine
   n. safety pins
   o. anitibacterial cream (Bacitracin)
2. Small towel, washcloth
3. Swimsuit
4. Swimmer's goggles
5. Tennis shoes
6. Shower sandals

Front Left Pannier
1. Food, food, food
2. Twelve plastic freezer bags, one-gallon size
3. Water bottles

Top of Rear Rack
1. Sleeping bag in stuff bag
2. Tent, ground cloth in stuff bag
3. Air mattress in stuff bag
4. Safety flags
5. Four 12-inch bungee cords, four 16-inch bungee cords
6. Lightweight camping chair (optional)
7. Fishing gear and pole (optional)
8. Spare tire or two (optional, but needed on international tour)

Day Pack or small backpack
1. Camera
2. Extra lens, spare camera battery
3. Cleaning equipment, brush, paper, fluid
4. Filters
5. Notebook and pen
6. Radio, headphones (optional)
7. Tape recorder (optional)
8. Cassettes (optional)
9. Cycling shoes
10. Helmet
11. Spare food
12. Malaria pills
13. Plane tickets
14. Spare batteries for light and recorder
15. Binoculars
16. Passport and pouch with money (optional location)
17. Shot record
18. Four ten-inch Velcro straps
19. Money belt
20. Small address book
21. Metric conversion card
22. Cable and combination lock

Camping Techniques

"Bicycle adventure: If a lone wolf lifts his plaintive call into the moonlight, you might call that adventure. While you're sweating like a horse in a climb over a 12,000-foot pass, that's an adventure. When howling head winds press your lips against your teeth, you're sure to be facing a mighty struggle. But that's not what makes an adventure. It's your willingness to conquer it, to present yourself at the doorstep of Nature. That creates the experience. No more greater joy can come from life than to live inside a moment of adventure. It is the uncommon experience that gives your life expectation."

The Gourmet Bicyclist,
looking at 20,300-foot Denali in Alaska, 1977

Camping And Cooking In Established Campgrounds

When you camp in an established campground, many obstacles are overcome immediately. You have a picnic table, water, washing facilities and seating area at your command. Nonetheless, you should buy food and load up on water two to three hours before sunset in case you don't reach an established campground. Always check your map for locations.

Making camp

After finding a spot in a campground – one to two hours before dark – you should:
- Pitch your tent on high ground.
- Roll out the sleeping mattress and sleeping bag.
- Place all your gear in the tent. Always put your gear in the same places, so you know where to find specific items, even in the dark. Always place your flashlight exactly in the same place so you can grab it when you need it.
- Make sure your "miner's" lamp is on your head and ready to work as darkness falls. These head lamps can be purchased in camping outlets. You might look like a coal miner walking around in the dark, but I find this lamp very useful.
- Remember not to place any food in your tent, especially in bear country. It should be placed in a food box, if available, or hung from trees as described in the section on camping in bear country. You can keep food in your tent if you're not in bear country, but never leave food in your tent unattended. You can leave food in your tent if you are sleeping, provided you're not in bear country.

- Lock your bike to a tree or to your helmet inside your tent. To do this, run the cable through the frame of your bike, then into your tent and lock it to your helmet strap. When you zip up the tent, the cable acts as an umbilical cord between it and your bike. If someone tries to make off with your cycle, they won't get far before you notice half your tent is being pulled away.
- Take out your candle lantern and light it on the table.
- Always light the match before turning on the gas to your stove. NEVER turn on the gas first, unless you want to make like a Saturn rocket and blast yourself to the moon.
- Set up your tablecloth.
- Take out your cutting board, utensils, pans, food, water bottles and spices.
- Prepare the meal.
- Enjoy!

Cooking and food storage

Before cooking your meal, make good use of the stove burner for heating water for tea or hot chocolate.

If you're cooking by campfire, let the wood burn down so you get an even heat from the coals. You'll also have to tackle the problem of balancing pots on the coals.

Once you've prepared the food for cooking by chopping and cutting, place the food into the cooking pot. As the dinner progresses, keep an eye on the food to keep it from burning.

After dinner, wash everything with soap and rinse with water. Leave no food out for the animals. Keep extra food in a locked food box – a wooden or metal box used in some campgrounds where animals are a concern. If there are no food boxes, and you're in bear or mountain lion country, do not store food in your tent. Hang it in a tree 300 feet from your camp.

Leave none of your gear out in the rain. Either store in the tent or use the vestibule of your tent to protect your gear.

Camping And Cooking In Primitive Areas

Camping in primitive (wilderness) areas presents several challenges that must be considered. You must be more responsible to your environment, (i.e., disposal of human waste, water contamination and generated food and paper waste). You are more susceptible to bears, raccoons, squirrels and wild pigs charging into your camp, looking for food. If it's a big old grizzly, he might be looking for you because he has a copy of *The Gourmet Bear In Search Of A Bicyclist*. Take precautions when camping in the wilds.

Again, make certain you have loaded up on extra water two to three hours before dusk. Or carry a filter that can purify water if there are ample places to fetch it – such as in the mountains or in lake regions.

Next, look for a campsite well off the road and hidden away from the sight of others. Not only is it a good idea to "vanish" into the wilderness for personal safety's sake, you will sleep better without hearing traffic all night.

Most dirt roads or trails on public land will lead to a hiding place. Try to get behind trees, brush, hills or a mountain. You want to be concealed from sight, along with your fire or candlelight.

Be certain to keep your tent away from fire. Ashes will burn through the nylon in seconds. Place your tent on high ground, so that if it rains, you won't wake up feeling like you're being swept over Niagara Falls. Special note: Eight out of ten persons reading this still will choose to learn this lesson the hard way! Trust me, you'll wake up in the middle of the night wishing you had gills…

Making Camp In Primitive Areas
- Secure food and one-and-a-half gallons of water two or three hours before dusk.
- Look for an abandoned road or trail and "vanish" into the landscape. Make camp one to two hours before dusk or sooner.
- Pitch your tent on high ground. The site should be safe from lightning and potential washout from a rainstorm.
- Roll out your air mattress and sleeping bag.
- Place all your gear in the exactly same place every night.
- Place your flashlight near your headrest, and secure your miner's lamp to your forehead before dark. Once your tent and gear is secured inside, either lock your bike to a tree or run the cable from the bike to your helmet inside your tent. That way, when you close the tent zipper, your bike can't go anywhere without your tent going with it.
- If you have a campfire, make sure it is 25 feet away from your tent. If that is not possible, use your stove for cooking.
- Spread your tablecloth on the ground outside your tent.
- Secure your candle lantern where you can use it.
- Organize all your cooking gear and food in front of you.
- If you're using a stove, make sure it's stable. You don't need a scalding injury while away from medical help.
- If you drink coffee, hot chocolate or tea, boil your water first.
- Prepare food. Cook food. Eat like a maniac!
- Wash dishes and clean up all traces of food.
- Always leave the bottom zipper of your tent open if you leave camp to take a bath or for any other reason. Whether you have food in

the tent or not, curious squirrels may bite their way through the nylon to see what's inside.

Building Campfires Safely In The Wilderness

If you enjoy ashes in your soup and burning embers in your potatoes, make yourself happy – cook on an open fire. It's primordial. Humans have been enjoying campfires before the wheel was invented. It beats watching television, unless you think watching *Roseanne* is a meaningful life experience.

You need to remember a few points about making a fire to keeps it safe and under control:

- Always check for – and obey – a no-burn rule. Use common sense when camping in a dry area.
- Build a protective rock ring around the fire. You can wet the ground around the fire ring if you have ample water.
- Keep the fire away from tents and other fabrics. Watch out for your Lycra or Gore-Tex. One flying ember will burn a hole in it.
- Keep your eyes on the fire at all times.
- Build the fire away from overhanging tree branches or dry brush. If you build under some low-hanging branches, you might turn the tree into a bonfire. Explain that to the local fire chief after you've taken her away from her husband and four kids at supper-time. (On second thought, maybe she wouldn't mind a little adventure away from hubby and the kids…) Finally, avoid building a fire against a large rock or cliff because it will leave unsightly smoke scars.
- Keep a water supply handy in case you need to douse the flames.
- Let the fire burn down before you place your pots into the embers. You want a slow, even heat for your food.
- If it's windy, eat pork and beans out of a can, or a sandwich. Avoid the chance of a runaway fire.
- Before hitting the sack, be certain to put the fire COMPLETELY OUT by smothering it with water or dirt.
- When finished with the fireplace, spread the rocks out and return the fire area to its natural appearance. Spread the ashes and place leaves and brush over the fire pit.

Fire In Your Tent

On those rainy or windy days, your first inclination might be to cook in your tent. Don't.

Okay, I know you're starving to death and you need something warm in your stomach. Again, don't cook in your tent.

There are so many little things that can, and will, go wrong when you have an open flame burning in your tent. I'm as careful as a person can be, but once, I nearly turned my tent into a bonfire! Avoid learning this lesson the hard way.

Candle Lantern

The only flame I allow in my tent is a glass and aluminum-encased candle lantern. Even then, I never leave it in the tent unattended. Make sure it's either hanging from the roof on a string, or resting on a flat surface (book or notepad).

Fire inside your tent is nothing to fool with, and that's not a lesson you want to learn the hard way.

Sanitation

It's very important to follow a few rules when camping in primitive wilderness situations:

When washing dishes, heat the water and use biodegradable soap. If you're washing in a lake or stream, make sure you discard the soapy water onto the soil at least 15 feet away from the lake or stream water so it drains into the ground. Rinse your cooking gear thoroughly.

Pack out what you pack in. I even pick up trash left by ignorant campers. I honor Nature by leaving a place cleaner than I found it. In the immortal words of Goethe, ''Do not think that you can do so little, that you do nothing at all.'' Avoid burning anything. Always take all your trash to a receptacle in the next town.

Since no toilets are available in primitive campsites, please follow strict wilderness rules:
- Find a spot 20 to 30 yards away from your campsite and away from a water source.
- Dig a hole four to six inches deep. Cover your waste with soil. If that is not possible, cover with a rock or leaves. Do not leave your toilet paper.
- You may burn your toilet paper in a campfire. If dry conditions exist or combustibles are present, wrap your used TP in plastic and carry it out with you.

In Chile, my friend Doug nearly burned an entire wheat field because th flame he used to burn his toilet paper ignited to the dry stalks. The next thing I know, Doug is waddling toward me with his shorts around his ankles, screaming, ''I just shit in the wrong place!'' We grabbed six water bottles and ran back to the fire, squirting it with our tiny water guns. A passing motorist and an old lady stopped to help us. You can imagine her shock and confusion when she saw Doug with his shorts at his ankles and me screaming and squirting water at the flames. She didn't know whether to help us or faint. Moral of this episode: Be careful where you strike a match to your toilet paper...and pull up your pants before you light it.

Cleaning And Hygiene

While on tour, you're living at a basic level. You're closer to being an animal than you've ever been. Bugs will try to invade your tent and mosquitoes will buzz around your head. Spiders will spin webs across your tent at night and they will be eating their "catch" when you step out the next day. You'll go to sleep under moonlight and wake up with the sun. The morning alarm clock might be the laughing call of an Australian kookaburra bird. It's natural, but it's dirty out there on a bike.

That's why you must maintain good sanitation and hygiene practices.

Wash your hands before preparing food. Be certain to use biodegradable soap. If you don't have any, use any soap, but make sure you use it. Avoid throwing soapy water into a stream or lake. Throw it onto the land where it can drain into the soil.

After any use of pots and pans, make certain to wash and rinse them. Use your camp towel to wipe them or let them dry in the sun.

Honor Nature and she will bless you with wonders at a round bend in the road.

Bear And Lion Country

"Bears are made of the same dust as we, and breathe the same winds and drink of the same waters. A bear's days are warmed by the same sun, his dwellings are overdomed by the same blue sky, and his life turns and ebbs with heart pulsings like ours. He was poured from the same first fountain. And whether he at last goes to our stingy Heaven or not, he has terrestrial immortality. His life, not long, not short, knows no beginning, no ending. To him life unstinted, unplanned, is above the accidents of time, and his years, markless and boundless, equal eternity."
John Muir, hiking in Yosemite Valley, California, 1838

Camping In Grizzly Or Black Bear Country

The grizzly is North America's symbol of wildness. His domain reaches from Yellowstone to Alaska. To catch a glimpse of this great animal is to fill your eyes with wonder. His wildness defines the wilderness. In his domain, he is king.

If you tour in the grizzly's realm, you need to understand how a grizzly operates. You want to tread carefully in his wilderness home.

Nothing will scare the daylights out of you faster than coming face to face with a bear. Few animals will kill you faster than a grizzly if she is so inclined. If she comes in the night, you will feel terror like never before because you have the added uncertainty of darkness. The sound of her grunting will drive your heart into a pumping frenzy, and your blood will race around your body like cars in the Indy 500.

I shivered in my sleeping bag while a grizzly dragged his muzzle across the side of my tent one morning in Alaska. His saliva left a mark on the nylon for a few weeks, and a mark for a lifetime in my mind. I'll never forget the three-and-a-half-inch claws that tore through the back of my tent...That day, I was lucky.

Bears are capricious, unpredictable and dangerous. They are always in search of food. Anything that looks edible to them is fair game. They eat berries, salmon, moose, mice and humans without discrimination.

That's why this chapter is devoted to camping in grizzly bear, black bear and mountain lion country.

If you ride your bicycle into remote regions in North America, or other areas of the world, sooner or late, you will camp in bear country. It's not something to be feared, but it is something you must respect. You are in his dining room.

The key to your safety and survival in Mr. Grizzly's domain is respect. You must honor the rules of the wilderness. You must follow those rules each and every time you camp. You may not get a second chance.

Imagine looking into a grizzly's eyes, backed by his 800 pounds of teeth and claws, and pleading, "Gee, Mr. Bear, could you just give me a break this time...I'm really sorry I left my chocolate chip cookies inside my tent...Can we make a deal, like, I'll give you my first-born child...Please sir, pretty please..."

Never ever assume a bear won't walk into your life.

At the same time, you can't camp in fear. During my journeys to Alaska, I have enjoyed extraordinary moments watching rogue grizzlies fishing for salmon and mother grizzlies playing with their cubs. It was a great wonder to see such incredible sights–from a distance.

I also have had the living hell scared out of me because of my own carelessness.

By using common sense and following the rules, you can minimize the chances and danger of a bear confrontation. But your safety cannot be guaranteed. You could do everything right, and still run into a bear–especially if he's trying to find food for his evening dinner!

However, since I've alarmed you, let me put this in proper perspective. If you follow Nature's rules, your chances of a bear confrontation are less than being hit by lightning. Therefore, go ahead and enjoy yourself. And if you do encounter a bear, you'll return home with great bear stories that will keep your friends glued to your every word.

Remember this: Bears are attracted to food smells, which makes them overcome their fear of humans. Be smart and keep food odor off your body and tent, and away from your camping area.

You've got adventure glued to your guts. Camping in bear country is part of bicycle touring.

Rules For Camping In Bear Country

Camp in an area least likely to be visited by a bear. Stay away from animal trails, large droppings, diggings, berry bushes, beehives and watering holes. Don't swim in streams where salmon are running. If you do, you may end up running for your own life.

Make absolutely certain your tent has no food odor in or on it. If you have spilled jam or peanut butter (grizzlies have grown accustomed to Skippy's Crunchy Style) on your tent fabric, wash it clean.

Cook 300 feet away from your tent. Wash your gear thoroughly. Do not sleep in the same clothes that were on your body while you were cooking dinner.

Make sure you avoid keeping perfume, deodorant or toothpaste in your tent. Keep anything that has an odor in your food bag and hang it away from your camp.

Hang your front food panniers in a strong 1.5-millimeter-thick plastic food bag at least 300 feet from tent. That means your camp, cooking and food-hanging areas are in a triangle 300 feet apart. (See Figure A.) If a bear does amble into your sector, he'll go after your food bag, and more than likely, he won't bother you.

Figure A

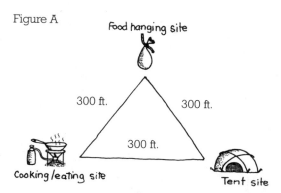

The Bear-Defense Triangle:

Your tent should be at least 300 feet from the cooking site and 300 feet from where you hang your food stores.

Bear-proof canisters that can carry several days of food supply, cost about $80 and can be purchased at many camping outlets. Carry it on the packs on top of your bike.

After you've hung your food, take out a wet cloth and wipe your face and hands to ensure you have no food odor on them.

Finally, brush and floss your teeth. You wouldn't want a tiny piece of food between your molars to be the reason you inadvertently invited Mr. Grizz to feast upon your body at night. Can you imagine the coroner's report in Whitehorse, Yukon…"Gourmet bicyclist was mauled last night because he left one little piece of fried chicken between his teeth…He could have starred in the movie *Dumb and Dumber*."

Also, remember to employ the same sanitation rules you learned in the primitive camping section.

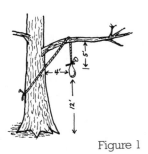

Figure 1

How To Hang Your Food:

Attach one end of a black parachute cord (to blend with the darkness) to a rock and throw it over a tree limb. Use the other end of the cord to tie your food bag. Pull the bag into the air at least 12 feet above the ground, at least five feet from the tree trunk and at least five feet from the limb where the cord is hanging.

Secure the parachute cord by tying it to a limb at the base of the tree or some other tree.

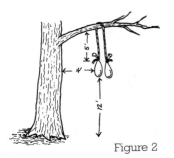

Figure 2

There is a second method for hanging food: Loop two bags over a limb so they balance each other and let them dangle with no tie-off cord. Some bears have figured out how to follow the tie-off cord and release it by batting or pawing it – mostly in places like Yosemite where so many careless campers visit. This second method should discourage a bear's efforts. However, I find it hard to hang the food using this method.

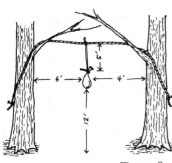

Figure 3

A third method is to throw a line over the branches of two trees about ten feet apart. Hang your food bag between the trees on the line.

Do what works best for you.

Grizzlies do not intentionally prey on humans. As long as they are not drawn to any food odor, you should enjoy a good night's sleep.

If A Bear Or Mountain Lion Should Confront You

Okay, you've followed the rules, but you wake up to the sounds of a bear outside your tent, or something else that's breathing and prowling through the night mist. Your nostrils fill with the stench of something that's got a really bad case of halitosis.

You don't have a gun, but you do have a Buck knife. If you used a gun on a grizzly, it would only piss him off. As for a knife, he'd snatch it out of your hands and use it as a toothpick afterwards. Maybe you have a pair of legs that can run like San Francisco 49er Jerry Rice? Most likely, you wish you were an eagle so you could fly away at that moment.

What To Do

Stay calm. Remember that bears and mountain lions don't like humans. It could be a deer, moose or elk. Unless you're in bear country in early spring, when a bear is just out of the den and hungry, he may only be curious and sniffing around.

I have been told that a good strategy is to play dead inside your sleeping bag if you're attacked by a grizzly. If you're with another person, you may opt to run in different directions. At least one of you would live. There are no hard and fast rules that guarantee anything in this situation.

During the day, be alert. If you come in contact with a grizzly, try to move out of his area. Never run. Make lots of noise by blowing on a whistle if you're hiking. If a bear sees you and charges, turn sideways and do not look at him. He may still attack you, but then again, if you are not threatening, he may not. If an attack is imminent, drop to the ground and assume a cannonball position with your hands over your head to protect your head and stomach.

If you run, he most likely will chase you down. At this juncture, you may want to...

...Pray. It may not do any good, but it may make you feel better. If your prayer isn't working, make a quick conversion to another religion and pray faster. If you die, you died while on an adventure, which makes it a bit heroic. It's better to die this way than suffering a heart attack while sprawled out on the easy chair with a remote glued to your hand.

When confronting a black bear, you have a much greater chance of survival. Stand your ground. Do not drop to the ground or play dead. Don't look into his eyes; stay on your feet and spread your arms a bit to present a larger presence. Don't look scared, even if you're wetting your pants with fear. Maintain your composure until the black bear leaves your area.

If confronted with a mountain lion or puma, stand your ground and make yourself appear larger if possible. Move away slowly. If you have a child with you, pick him or her up and hold the child close to you. With a cat, you can fight back and it may run away. If also may run if you throw rocks at it. Do not run yourself. Again, it's between you and lady luck.

There is one thing you can count on while on tour. Anything can happen. Adventure is not always comfortable, but it is still adventure. I'm a firm believer that neither bliss or adventure are ever obtained by staying home in your rocking chair.

Jack London said it best when he wrote: "I would rather be ashes than dust. I would rather my spark burn into a brilliant blaze. I would rather be a superb meteor, every atom of me in magnificent glow–than a sleepy, permanent planet. Man's chief purpose is to live, not exist. I shall not waste my days trying to prolong them. I will use my time."

As a final note, be confident that you will make your way through bear country safely if you will follow the rules of Nature. When you respect Nature, that respect will be given back to you.

I can see you sitting around the table with your friends after your tour in Alaska.

"Yeah, I woke up one morning on the Kenai River when I heard a blood-curdling growl...I thought the sun was shinning through my mosquito netting, but it was the pearly whites of a thousand-pound grizzly...Well sir, I didn't have much time to think, so I pulled out my Bowie Knife – kinda like Daniel Boone – and stared back into that grizzly's eyes...That's when I gave him a toothy growl of my own...It scared him so badly, he scrambled up a tree, where we used him for an umbrella to keep that 24-hour sun from burning down on us while we ate fresh salmon steaks on the campfire..."

Jack London would have been proud.

International Touring

"There can only be one way through the ring of life. It's a constant spiritual move-ment toward self-fulfillment through growth of the mind and expansion of the sens-es. It's ceaseless and constant throughout one's life."
The Gourmet Bicyclist at the Wall of China,1984

When riding outside the grocery-store-and-fast-food borders of the United States, you open yourself up to new culinary challenges and dan-gers. In America, you can count on clean water. Meats are inspected by the U.S. Department of Agriculture. You can count on most people speak-ing English, except in California, where dozens of languages exist. The roads are smooth and the living is easy.

You're sick of it, right? Too many motor home mentalities! Cable TV hookups in campsites. Every town in America looks like every other town. First you see the Golden Arches, followed by Wendy's, Subway, Arby's and Pizza Hut. Everybody walking out of a fast-food restaurant looks like they need special coaching by Richard Simmons or Jenny Craig. Ye gads! What ever happened to regional flavor, small town diners, personal dress and style? Does anyone remember what an old-time hardware store smells like? Do they know the wooden floors creak? Not a chance.

Sounds like you're ready to see how the other 95% live. Hold onto your handlebars and pull up your Lycra shorts because you're in for one heck of a surprise.

Do not ever underestimate your potential circumstances on tour. Be smart. Be prepared. Your life may depend on your thoughtful and measured actions. You can't hope someone will rescue you like they do in the movies.

Anytime you ride into a foreign country, you're subject to conditions you won't find at home. You may be vulnerable to infectious diseases, tainted food and water. You need extra precautions with eating, drinking and medicine.

Riding Outside The United States

While on tour in any one of the more than 180 countries around the world, you will notice many differences. The freedoms you take for grant-ed at home. may be turned upside down in China. The way people dress on the altiplano (treeless land above 12,000 feet in Bolivia) is different from the natives in Brazil. People in the Middle East bow to Allah five times a day and the women are covered except for their eyes. Australia's kangaroos may enthrall you with their 40-foot leaps. Europe's architecture and history will seduce you. The cultures, languages, animals and people you visit will change dramatically from border to border. Your patience and understanding will be challenged often in foreign lands.

However, people the world over are friendly and helpful. They laugh, cry and struggle through different parts of their lives, just like you do. It is the village of humanity in which you travel.

Along the way, you will need to adapt. That is the key to your success. When it comes to eating, you're in for challenges and fabulous experiences.

First, you're 90% certain of suffering from food poisoning or a bacterial disruption of your stomach or colon. Whether it's a giardia cyst, worms, dysentery, hepatitis or food poisoning – you're headed for the bathroom. The key is: accept its inevitability, endure it, and get on with your tour. Take along medicine for diarrhea and pills to kill parasites. Get the medications at your doctor's office.

Water On International Tours

The primary concern on international tours is water. The rules are simple:
- Always filter your water.
- Use purification tablets to ensure safety.

Make certain when you're filtering water to avoid mixing droplets of unfiltered water with filtered water. Just one unfiltered droplet can cause you sickness. That's why a purification tablet is your second line of defense in making your water safe.

No matter how much time it takes to filter water, do it painstakingly. It can mean the difference between miles of smiles and days of lying on your back with giardia making your colon feel like it's an arena for a bumper-car rally.

Diseases

Several diseases await you while on tour in Third World countries. Be prudent and you will save yourself from most of them. Take every preventative shot in the book to protect yourself. Your physician can provide the immunizations for you.

Hepatitis

Infectious hepatitis is one heck of a nasty problem in the Third World. To combat it, I take gamma-globulin shots that last up to six months. So far, so good. Make sure you take the shot several weeks before the trip, and don't take a shot of gamma-globulin with any live virus vaccines. Give yourself a two-week interval between the vaccines. Your doctor should remind you of this.

If you get hepatitis, you'll feel like someone used your body as a practice target for a bow and arrow. You will be weak, your eyes will turn yellow, and your urine will darken.

You can get hepatitis from food or water. If you come down with it, see a doctor as quickly as possible.

Diarrhea/Dysentery

The Inca Two-Step, or Montezuma's Revenge, are two other names for this affliction. We call it diarrhea in the United States, but it takes on a whole new meaning in the Third World. You literally will spend entire days on the toilet. If you find blood in your feces, along with experiencing cramps in the stomach, it could be dysentery. You may need to take tetracycline. See a doctor.

Upon returning from any international tour, have your feces and urine checked for bugs.

Transporting Food Over Long Distances

One of your biggest challenges will be transporting food and water across long stretches of desert or uninhabited mountains. Be sure to look at a map and find out how far it is to the next food and water. We have carried as much as six days of food with us when we rode from La Paz, Bolivia to Arica, Chile. Our bikes looked more like pack mules than touring machines.

Our supplies included six days worth of oatmeal, dried beans and rice, dried breads and rolls, canned tuna, dried fruits, potatoes, carrots and onions, and other such sturdy, non-perishable foods. With rice, beans and oatmeal, you'll power yourself anywhere.

In desert situations, like in the Atacoma Desert of Chile, or the Sahara in Africa, you're looking at hundreds of miles of sand. You won't see a fly or mosquito. You will need to bring five gallons of water with you to ensure making it to the next roadhouse. That's especially important on the Nullabor Plains (treeless) in the Outback of Australia, where temperatures reach 110 degrees Fahrenheit and higher. The sun sucks water out of your skin like a wet-vac vacuum. I've toured through 100 miles of Death Valley at 114 degrees F (190 degrees at ground level). I drank five gallons of water in one day, and I never went to the bathroom.

Other considerations:

As stated earlier, you should boil, use drops or filter your water, and eat only cooked foods. Always peel fruits and vegetables. You might consider becoming a temporary vegetarian once you see how dairy products and meats are left out in the sun with flies crawling on them.

Because you will not be able to bathe every day, carry antifungal ointment. Take a wash cloth and wipe yourself down nightly with filtered water from your bike bottles. This will help prevent fungal growth on your skin. For poison ivy or other skin rashes, carry cortizone cream.

Your passport is vulnerable to theft. Always keep it and money on your person, in a pouch around your neck or in your pack. Your day pack should always go with you on a break, or have a trusted friend watch your gear while you go to the rest room.

During a tour in foreign countries, preventive maintenance is very important. Check your spokes often and take plenty of spare nuts and bolts. Two spare tubes and one extra tire are a minimum. Carry enough patch gear for 20 punctures. You will need a freewheel pulling wrench and a half-dozen spare spokes. Carry an extra chain, chain breaker and rear derailleur. In Third World countries, strongly consider a mountain bike converted for touring (i.e., put drop bars on it and ride with 1.95-inch tires with a minimum of 36 and up to 40 spokes (if you're heavier than 190 pounds) on the rear 26-inch rim. A combination road/dirt tire works well. For mountainous countries, try a 22 to 32 tooth rear sprocket ratio (front to back) for your lowest gear.

There's a reason you're traveling along adventure highway. As John Muir wrote, "Camp out among the grass and gentians of glacier meadows, in craggy garden nooks full of Nature's darlings. Climb the mountains and get their good tidings. Nature's peace will flow into you as sunshine flows into trees. The winds will blow their own freshness into you, and the storms their energy, while cares will drop off like autumn leaves."

Be smart. Stayed prepared. Enjoy the peace and silence.

A Baker's Dozen

"Your legs feel like fried bacon after a day of climbing and descending. It's a roller coaster ride, but no one is pulling you up the mountain. You're headed toward Yosemite more than 6,500 feet of pounding the pedals. You're aware of every movement because your thighs feel tender with a kind of pain. You push on, toward the final ascent into the valley. In front of you is a monster mountain – El Capitan. Suddenly, you feel only wonder."

The Gourmet Bicyclist riding into Yosemite Valley, 1995

What's A Baker's Dozen?

In earlier times, patrons of local merchants could count on personal service from retailers who knew customers' names and always had a friendly smile. It was good business to please the patrons. Proprietors developed personal techniques to get the customer to come back to their stores.

Bake shops used a technique that was certain to please large-volume buyers. When customers ordered a dozen loaves of bread, the baker added one more as a bonus. It was called a "Baker's Dozen."

A Baker's Dozen of Touring Tips

You will develop dozens of personal habits while touring. Your gear will be placed where you want it and you will evolve an almost ritualistic style of doing things.

Of course, the most important thing you can do is buy a good bike and have a touring veteran fit it to your body. Have the bike fitted at three junctures:

- Seat to pedal height. Your hips should remain stable while pedaling.
- Knee to pedal axle. You should be able to drip a plumb line straight from the back of your patella to the axle of the pedal.
- Length from your seat to the handlebars.

I would buy a bike from a store where you will get good service. If you buy mail order, be sure you know what you're doing or have a friend who knows what he or she is doing help you select the best bike.

I'd like to share a baker's dozen of touring tips to make your journey easier and safer:

1.   No matter how little or how much you ride, some day you are going to take a fall. Since you don't know how serious that fall will be, you must anticipate the worst and think about your head. It is the most vulnerable part of your body in an accident. If you hit the cement, your head will crack like a raw eggshell. The more than 50,000 bicycle accidents in the United States each year are a good reason to wear head protection. Always wear a helmet and have it cinched when you ride. Buy a helmet that meets the ANSI standard and look around until you find one that fits you comfortably. Make sure it has an easy latch chin strap. For protection from the sun, buy a wide-billed visor and fit it to your helmet. Many good helmets putout by Giro, Bell, Specialized and others.

2.   Buy the best sunglasses you can afford to protect your eyes. You will protect yourself from deadly radiation coming through the diminished ozone layer and from possible injury from flying rocks, straw and sand. Have a string to hold them around your neck. My sunglasses are a pair of $100 Glacier Goggles from Bausch and Lomb. They wear like iron and protect your eyes from dangerous ultraviolet rays.

3.   Buy an excellent pair of shoes designed specifically for bicycle touring. You need the strong metal or plastic shank along the foot bed to give you balanced application of your whole foot to the pedal. Without a good shoe, your foot will suffer more pressure pain than you can imagine. Always tie the shoelaces on your right shoe off to the side so you won't get them caught in the chain. Again, buy a shoe that fits your foot comfortably. Go to a local bike shop, or if you don't have one in town, check with Performance, Bike Nashbar and other mail-order outfits.

4.   Learn how to maintain and repair your bicycle. Take a bicycle repair course with hands-on instruction. You must be able to take apart the wheel hubs, bottom bracket, head tube and freewheel assembly. You need to know how to adjust the brakes and derailleur systems. Make sure you know how to correct a rim when it is out of true. If you're on a world tour, you need to be able to rebuild a rim. You must know how to repair a tube and tire. Check all the spokes and nuts and bolts on your bike daily. It's simple to do and will save you big headaches because you will catch a problem before it has a chance to grow worse. Take all the tools you need to break down your bike.

5.   Your nutrition on a bike trip is important. Stay as close to a high-carbohydrate diet as possible. You will gain more stamina, power and endurance from pasta, grains, fruits, cereals, vegetables and breads. I've been a vegetarian for 19 years and maintain excellent health. If you eat

animal protein, your system works harder to digest and use the nutrients. You may build up fats and cholesterol, and consume many chemicals. In a Third World country, you're playing a dangerous game with food poisoning and other diseases when you consume flesh and dairy products. Be sure to peel fruits before you eat them. You may want to take a supply of multiple vitamin and minerals on an extended tour. Your body suffers considerable depletion of resources while pedaling. Keep eating all the time.

6.   Keep your body covered while touring. Buy a light-colored shirt that covers your neck and arms. You might consider wearing light-colored tights to reflect heat and protect you from the sun. Long hours of touring will burn the skin and create a playground for skin cancer. Zinc oxide your lips and use sun block on your face and hands.

7.   Drink water constantly. You're better off drinking water than any other liquid. While in Third World countries, be sure you filter and treat the water. If you drink water tainted with a couple of nasty bacteria or flukes, you're going to be sick.

8.   While touring in a mountainous region, be sure to allow your body to acclimate itself to the elevation. If not, you could suffer altitude sickness. If you push too high too fast, you could die of pulmonary edema. If you feel weak, short of breath and start coughing, drop below 10,000 feet and stay there for a few days until you feel well enough to climb again. Cerebral edema is a more serious sickness because it affects your brain. You will suffer a pounding headache and possible double vision. If you do not take action, death could result. Descend below 10,000 feet immediately and get medical attention.

9.   When taking airlines and trains to major destinations, you'll have to box your bike for transport. Go to a bicycle shop and pick a box to fit your bike out of their dumpster, or ask them to save you one. Additionally, railroads offer bike boxes. (See Breaking Down And Packing Your Bike For Airline Travel.)

10. You are going to attract lots of attention while on tour and many people will invite you into their homes. I have never had a problem, but you need to be cautious, especially if you are a woman. You might accept lodging only if you meet a family or couple. I would shy away from persons who look suspicious.

Men may have a faster cadence and move ahead of a woman partner. This is important: If you're on tour with your wife or a female companion, ride behind her so you stay together. If you pedal too far ahead, she will feel alone and vulnerable. She will become highly agitated given enough time, and your relationship will suffer – along with your tour. Trust me on this one, guys!

11. Dogs can be the bane of your bicycling tour. They will frighten the daylights out of you and worse, bite you. You could be sent to the hospital for stitches or rabies shots. If a dog or dogs attack, they usually bark first so you know they are coming. It's worth your efforts to deal with their attacks quickly. Always be alert for dogs by keeping an eye on a house or any area you think has dogs. If you can outrun dogs by pedaling past their territory, go for it. You can carry a two-foot piece of fiberglass rod in your front rack to whip them with, or you can carry a can of dog repellent. The whip will keep them away most of the time, and you may run out of repellent at the most inopportune time. If pressed, carry a few stones in your handlebar bag and throw them at the dogs. As a last resort, you can get off your bike and walk behind it as you move out of their territory.

12. Always be prepared for survival situations by carrying ample water, food and shelter. Carry minimum amounts of food that will keep you fed for up to five days in remote regions. Keep a supply of oatmeal, rice and lentils for survival eating as a last resort. Make sure you can stay warm in a summer blizzard at high altitude by carrying a long-sleeved turtleneck undershirt made from a high-tech wicking/insulating fiber like Thermax, a wool sweater, warm tights and a waterproof/breathable (Gore-tex) jacket. Mittens and waterproof covers will keep your hands warm.

13. Never ride at dusk or at night unless it is absolutely necessary. For an emergency situation, carry front and rear lights, and preferably a blinking strobe light attached to your traffic-side arm.

Breaking Down and Packing Your Bike For Airline Travel

Break your bike down by taking off the handlebars, front wheel, pedals, seat and pulling off the rear derailleur. Take the rear derailleur off the dropout, tape it to the chain and encase it in a cloth. (Do not forget this, or you'll suffer a bent dropout hanger and possibly a broken rear derailleur.) Lock the front dropouts with a steel axle pin or tape a block of wood or plastic between the front dropouts so the forks won't get bent during rough handling. Secure all nuts and bolts and pack the bike in paper so it won't move. The front wheel will fit beside the frame. Slip a piece of cardboard between the wheel and your bike so it won't suffer scratches. Everything you can do to keep the bike locked solidly still in the box is important.

Last But Not Least

The best advice I can give in this baker's dozen of touring tips is to be certain to have an orange flag on a erect six-foot long fiberglass pole locked to the struts on your rear rack. This makes you highly visible to motorists. A second flag on a three-foot fiberglass pole should be attached to the traffic side of your bike to protect you from being skimmed by cars.

The total effect is two orange, flapping flags that can be seen a half-mile away. They get the attention of approaching drivers both front and rear. When you have their attention, you are less likely to suffer consequences. You must remember that you might be sharing the road with at least 2,000 pounds of steel going at 55 miles per hour. Just one yawn or sneeze, a glance back at the kids, or a daydream could have a car running up the back of your panniers. Those flags are your life line to safety. Use them as if your life depended on them. Buy them at K-Mart or Target.

Finally, remember you're on adventure highway. You're an ambassador for your state or country. What you do affects others. Things you say and do last a lifetime to those you encounter. Make your tour a positive experience for all you meet. You will be rewarded with magical moments that last a lifetime in your heart and mind.

Romantic Modifications To Your Candle Lantern

"Wine is sunlight, held together by water."

Galileo

Romance flourishes all over the world. No matter what country, culture or political system—romance lives in the human heart. Almost always, it starts with food. Eating brings joy and enhances romantic ambiance.

Years ago, I pedaled through Switzerland. Drenched from an all-day drizzle, my girlfriend and I were miserable. We stopped in a quaint tavern in Gumligen, a small town outside Berne. It was right out of a Pinocchio movie. A fire crackled in the center of a big dining room. Red-and-white checkered cloths covered every table. Centered on top of each table, a single rose set the tone for romance, and beside it, a candle lantern flickered quietly.

We stood just inside the door, sopping wet. Several patrons looked up from their dinners, but quickly returned to their conversations. We smiled at them.

"You are Americans?" the hostess asked, walking up.

"Yes ma'am," I said.

"Right this way," she said, leading us toward the fireplace.

Fifteen minutes later, as we sipped red wine, the chef and his two daughters walked out with violins. They strode toward us with the certain intention of driving away the rain we had endured. They raised the instruments to their necks. We toasted them. They smiled. Their bows swept across the strings.

The music, combined with dancing flames from the hearth, quickly warmed our spirits. They played to us as if we were the only lovers in the world.

Later, they invited us into their home for hot baths and dry bed sheets. It was a night I shall remember for the rest of my life.

But the joy of that evening was even more appreciated because it was one of countless romantic moments I've enjoyed while bicycle touring. There is something special about touring cyclists. We are unique. Because we are unconventional, people react to us in diverse ways. Sometimes it turns into a flirtatious romance.

I admit it. I am a romantic. Taking my lady with me on tour is a time for special moments. The opportunities abound. Woman have the same opportunity to embellish romance as men do. It's a state of mental inclination.

However, romance can not be forced. The key is to see what it might "become." I don't mind sharing a secret with you – food is the great aphrodisiac. However, on a bicycle tour, many other factors work their way into the equation.

After a hard day of riding, I can use my candle lantern to go down to the lake to take a bath. My lady brings the soap and towels. The moon throws at sparkling path of light across the water. I set the candle lantern on a log. The rest is simple.

Have you ever watched the western horizon turn into a blazing sky-fire? It happens every night somewhere in the world. On tour, you will see sunsets beyond your imagination. You will be there because you followed your dreams.

Often, your candle lantern will light your campsite. By listening quietly, you may notice a symphony of crickets or the hootie-hoot-hoot of an owl. On some distant hill, a coyote, called a 'song dog' by the Indians, raises his head for a lonesome howl at the moon. Romance is modified by the inclinations of your mind.

Romance is simple. You light your candle lantern and hang it from the center of your tent. That one little light is enough to read an entire romance novel – or live it!

While preparing food over your stove, the night sky slowly turns to starlight. The steam escaping from your cooking pot brings tantalizing aromas to your nostrils. You light your candle lantern and wait for the simmering cuisine. Your companion walks up behind you and gives you a shoulder massage. A kind of ecstasy overcomes your soul.

At sunset, as the last "honk" comes from a gaggle of geese on the lake you're camping near, you and your companion are sitting by the campfire. The embers dance in all directions while the smoke curls peacefully upward through the pines. Your bodies feel exhausted, but your spirits soar on the silent night breezes. Your boyfriend reaches for your hand. You squeeze his, then look into his eyes with a smile. The dancing flames reflect in his eyes. You kiss. The candle lantern flickers on the log behind you. At that moment, you are at peace with the world – your eyes are closed and your spirit is open – to romance.

You both may be sitting by a river as the sun goes down. Between you is a stump. On top of it is your candle lantern and a bottle of sparkling wine. The sky is gold. Your hearts are melting. The day's ride was good. You pour into his cup. He tastes it. You want to taste him. He leans over the candle lantern to kiss you. The river flows quietly past you as an owl looks down from a distant tree. The two of you embrace under a million twinkling stars. At that moment, you are one with the universe.

Have you ever rode your touring bikes to the Grand Canyon? It is an experience of a lifetime. Years ago, on a cross-continent tour, my girl-friend and I rode to the edge of the canyon near Mather Point. From there, the canyon drops one mile to the Colorado River. We reached the edge near dusk. It was a time when the sky turned red against the golden rocks, and pink against the billowing white clouds. We grabbed our candle lantern and headed for a place where we could watch the sky effervesce into a rainbow of colors. When we reached the edge, a few scrub trees shielded us from the highway and other tourists.

We were alone as we dangled our feet over the edge of a mile-deep cliff. With the passing seconds, the light vanished into darkness and the stars twinkled across the vastness of space. Below us, a million years of erosion had transformed the rocks into unimaginable beauty. Beside us, our candle lantern flickered brightly into the universe. She held my hand. We kissed.

I'm a firm believer in romance. Poet Rod McKuen said, "I've been gone a long time now, and along the way, I've learned some things...you have to make the good times yourself...take the little times and make them big times...and save the times that are all right for the ones that aren't so good."

While on tour, your life is simple and purposeful – and above all, it's happy. For so many, that elusive quality of their lives seems like a dream. Every day on a bicycle tour, happiness comes with the territory. It may be the greatest secret touring cyclists possess.

While bicycle touring, you can make many modifications to your candle lantern. Its tiny flame of light can illuminate the path in front of you. Its simpleness will be a guide for your spirit. You may be having a conversation with someone from another country. Your flickering candle lantern will light your faces against the darkness. No matter where you are in the world, another cyclist is rolling toward you, ready to share his or her story with you. You share an extraordinary bond – bicycle touring. That cyclist's candle lantern will bring a new friendship into your life.

As you sit in the darkness, somewhere in the world, after a gourmet dinner, the quiet creates enchantment. You might be gazing across a river valley or into a fire. No matter where you are, a certain kind of magic inspires your life.

"What a privilege to know the profound stillness
and the peace of the land,
to see
star spangled skies,
and to listen to the pulse of the universe."

Jill Tremain

In the end, you will be modified by your candle lantern's warmth and light. Amour, amour, mon ami.

Part Two
Food On Tour

Cooking Equipment

"We need the tonic of the wilderness, to wade sometimes in the marsh where the bitten and the meadow hen lurk, and hear the booming of the snipe; to smell the whispering sedge where only some wilder and more solitary fowl builds her nest, and the mink crawls with its belly close to the ground."

Henry David Thoreau

Utensils

The key to success in cooking while touring is a good set of utensils. The proper tools will make food preparation safe, simple and efficient. As with everything "on tour," you need equipment that is light and sturdy. Avoid utensils that are heavy. Your friends may be excited about your heroic efforts, but your legs will give you their opinion on a climb over a 10,000-foot pass! With an overloaded bike, you will feel more like a pack mule than a touring cyclist.

Pack the following items:

- Carry a Swiss Army knife with multiple instruments. You can cut, clip and peel fruit with a good knife. Additionally, it doubles as a bottle and can opener. Couples should buy one with a corkscrew. Be prepared for those sunset moments on a quiet lake with the campfire licking the evening air. A fine wine makes for a romantic nightcap.
- Carry a plastic handled, stainless steel potato/carrot peeler. It's good for peeling other vegetables as well.
- Take a camping-quality plastic knife, fork and spoon. The knife is good for spreading peanut butter, mustard, margarine and jam. The knife and spoon double as stirring sticks.
- Bring a camping pot-and-pan combo and cover. Make sure you buy a set with copper bottoms for more uniform heating of food. Make sure you include one or two plastic coffee cups. They can double as one-cup measuring devices. Because these are the '90s, and there are an increasing number of potential partners solo touring, carry a second cup. You would hate to miss an opportunity to share a cup of tea or hot chocolate with someone special because you left the second cup home.
- For women on tour: Don't worry. Some fanciful guy will walk over to your campsite and say, "I'm a Gourmet Bicycle Chef. How would you like to taste my chicken cacciatore over a bed of sauteed mushrooms and rice?"

"Yeah, but I'm not sure you'll be able to keep up with me tomorrow…"

- In addition to the pot-and-pan combo, some riders carry a small eight-inch Teflon frying pan. They use it to cook pancakes, bacon and eggs. It also heats evenly. You might work this item into your cooking equipment if you don't mind the weight.
- Carry a strong sponge/scrubber combination and biodegradable soap.
- Carry a plastic spatula for flipping pancakes, burgers and fried potatoes.
- Carry a candle lantern and plenty of nine-hour candles (or oil).
- Carry a 10-inch round, or 10x9-inch oblong plastic cutting board. It's handy for chopping onions, carrots, cucumbers, potatoes and tomatoes. The plastic board is easy to pack and weighs no more than a hummingbird you might see on a summer morning.
- Cut a tablecloth to a 40x40-inch piece, or cut a piece of 1.25-millimeter plastic to the same specifications. You will be able to use it on

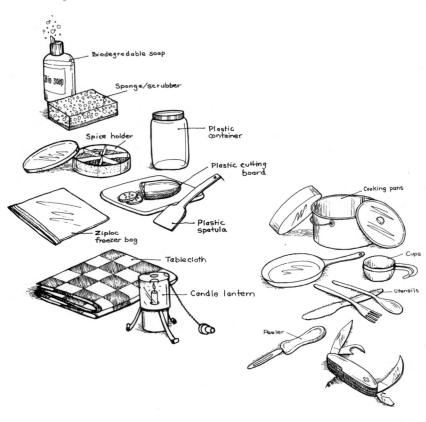

picnic tables, on the ground or in your tent. Be sure to wipe it clean after each meal.

- Bring a small packet of pre-moistened towelettes, or two hand towels.
- Carry four plastic containers with screw-on lids for tomatoes, avocados and peaches. If screw-on lids can't be found, you may have to opt for snap-on lids.
- Bring four plastic containers with screw-on lids for liquids and jams. Sizes vary from 8 to 16 ounces. Carry several four-ounce plastic jars with screw-on lids for spices.
- Carry one dozen gallon-size freezer bags (Ziploc bags work well). They're excellent for making sure things don't leak.
- Carry a six-section plastic spice jar. This can be purchased in most camping stores and comes with leak-proof snap lids.

Where To Buy Utensils

Scraping burned eggs or oatmeal off the bottom of a thin aluminum frying pan or pot isn't the way to start off a day of touring. At the same time, lugging a bulky Teflon frying pan up an 7% grade for five miles, along with the rest of your gear, is a challenging task.

The compromise for many riders is a stainless steel, copper-based pot and pan cooking system with detachable handles. In some cases, you can buy a good system with attached handles. Carry hard plastic cups or light metal ones that pack inside your pots.

Buy your utensils at an Army/Navy Surplus store or any fine camping outlet such as L.L. Bean, Eastern Mountain Sports, REI, Camping World, Campmor or Early Winters. These retailers carry top-quality gear that will perform year after year. If you plan to use your pans over open fires, you can either use liquid soap to make them more soot proof, or you may tire of the hassle, leave the pot black and enclose it in a gallon freezer bag or a nylon stuff bag. Additionally, a new product called a "heat diffuser plate" may give you better heat control over a fire.

Stoves

Camp stoves are the safest and easiest way to cook your food. You have dozens from which to choose.

Stability is key when looking for a cooking stove. You don't want your lap to become the landing pad for boiling water that tipped over because the stove's base was inadequate. Scalding water could end your bike tour.

Second, heating capability is important. Ideally, buy a stove that has variable flame control. If you're in the United States or other developed countries, you can buy butane cartridge burners that burn clean and cause no hassles. You can buy canisters at any K-Mart, Target or Wal-Mart. A GAZ stove is one of the easier units to buy and keep supplied, but the canisters are wasteful, don't work well in cold weather and are more expensive. There are many others from which you may choose.

For a detailed comparison of stoves, check with any of the fine camping stores mentioned in the back of this book for a stove comparison chart. Matching your needs with a stove will ensure you the best choice.

If you ride with a system using canisters, carry one in the stove and two extra cartridges at all times. Otherwise, you will be eating oatmeal soaked in cold water for dinner. It's amazing what you will eat when you're starving.

Stoves that operate on liquid fuel have the disadvantage of potential spillage. Remember to keep the storage bottle in the upright position at all times. Some riders place it on the underside of the down tube in the water bottle rack. Others place it in the rear pocket of the back pannier. For added protection against spillage, seal it in a one-gallon plastic freezer bag.

Third, fuel availability is very important. If you're pedaling a Third World tour, or up the Alaska Highway, you need a stove that burns whatever fuel is available. The MSR Whisperlight International or XGK are excellent for their versatility – you can burn nearly any kind of fuel in these stoves. Even though they don't possess good flame control, it is imperative that you carry this kind of stove on international tours.

Fourth, look at size and weight economy. You want a stove that is easy to pack and weighs as much as a feather – or is as light as possible. Be sure to buy a ditty bag to keep the stove, along with a lighter or matches, all in one place.

Fifth, look for dependability. Buy quality equipment and it will serve you well. Your stove should be light, easy to operate, easy to fuel, easy to clean and easy to pack. That stove will cook sumptuous dinners and heat hundreds of cups of hot chocolate or coffee on your bicycle tours. It's very important to buy a good one.

Campfires

Your second source of cooking heat is a campfire. If you're one of those "Rambo types" who enjoys ashes in your coffee and burning embers on your steak, a campfire is the answer.

Some tips:
- Let the wood burn down so you get an even heat from the coals.
- Work out a method for balancing your pot on the coals.
- Keep an eye on the food to keep it from burning, since the heat from a campfire is difficult to regulate.

Cooking At Altitude

When you're cooking at 5,000 feet and higher, you may have a few concerns, but for the most part, just keep in mind that you have to cook the food until it is ready. It takes twice as long to boil water for every increase of 5,000 feet. Your meal cooking time will extend as you ride higher.

I once was caught in a summer blizzard on a 16,000-foot pass in the Andes. I thought I was going to die of hypothermia before my soup warmed up enough for me to eat. (I cooked it in the vestibule area outside my tent.) I huddled in my sleeping bag until the soup was ready. When it finally got hot, I savored every sip as I watched the whiteout swirling outside my tent flaps. All I could think about was a hot tub back home, but for the time being, the hot soup had to do.

Carbohydrates are more easily absorbed at high altitude than proteins and fats, so go heavy on them. Keep hydrated. If you feel cramps, drink more water.

Buying and Carrying Food

"Time means nothing now. It slips away as easily as grains of sand on a wind-swept beach. But those grains only trade places. On my bike, I change the same way—new locations in the passage of time. The pedaling is incidental—like breathing. The hills and mountains come and go—my legs powering over them in a kind of winsome trance. Grappling with headwinds only brings determination, while riding a tail wind brings ecstasy. There is a transformation into a state of bliss, much like a sea gull gliding on the updrafts. I see them standing on the beaches or soaring over the waves. Just living. Just being. Me too."

**The Gourmet Bicyclist, along the Princess Highway,
south of Sydney, Australia, 1985**

Buying Groceries

If you're hungry, what you see is what you want. Wanting turns into buying, and what you buy is what you carry.

Think simple and compact. Purchase instant oatmeal, raisins in eight packs or canisters. Regardless of the length of your trip or the distance between grocery stores, you need to carry four to six breakfasts with you. The food weighs very little, yet provides "emergency" fuel for your body. The new oatmeal brands with freeze-dried strawberries, bananas and blueberries are excellent.

Whether you're buying for breakfast, lunch or dinner, you need to plan ahead. How far is the next city where you can stock up? Where can you find fresh vegetables? How do you keep meat from spoiling before dinner?

You have several choices when buying foods. You can stock up on many items from a supermarket – the lowest prices are at large chains that buy in quantity, and their big advantage is that they offer everything from A to Z.

Small-town grocery stores will carry many things you need, but they do not have large selections, nor do they always carry fresh vegetables. However, they make up for the deficiencies in other areas.

One of the nice things about small-town groceries is the possibility of meeting local characters. I met Joe and Mabel as I was cycling through a town in central Louisiana. He was munching on a bag of salty chips when Mabel chastised him, "...You're dumb for killing yourself eating that junk food."

Joe was 86 years old. He wasn't worried about dying, and kept on munching.

Then Mabel told me, "I was the oldest of 11 kids. I took care of them when my mom died…then I married Joe…I didn't know any better so I've been takin' care of him his whole life."

Joe looked up, grinned a ventilated smile and said, "There, you see, I ain't so dumb after all."

Another man, wearing tattered clothes and sporting holes in his shoes, stopped me in front of an old mercantile store in Mississippi.

"Ever change the oil in yore knees?" he asked.

Dumbfounded, I replied, "Only when they squeak."

He laughed. Josh was 91 years old and the son of a slave. For several hours, I listened to this ancient man. He possessed more 'real' knowledge about the civil war than a history book. Josh, with clouded eyes, yet a clear mind, captivated me. He departed with his 71-year-old son, or I would have listened to him into the evening.

Places To Find Fresh Food

Produce stands are a great place to buy food at its freshest. Stands along the highway offer vegetables, juices and fruits. The prices are rock bottom, and the carrots and potatoes may have been in the ground that morning. You might even find a gallon of freshly squeezed apple cider.

Buy food in the morning, or at least three hours before camp time. You want to avoid being in a panic as darkness is falling because you are out of food.

For my own peace of mind, I carry enough food to keep pedaling for two days without refills while on tour in America. In Third World countries or for other touring, I check a map to determine how far the next food source is, and plan on carrying up to six days of food or more.

High Energy Foods

"Screamers, hurtful burning screamers…what's that pain in my thighs?" You can sing those words to the tune of Super Tramp's "Dreamer." It's caused by lactic acid build-up.

On a bicycle tour, you're looking for foods that will power you through the day. You want "jet fuel" foods, meaning you want the greatest amount of energy with the fewest consequences. You may want to avoid lactic acid build-up, which makes your legs sore, or too many fats, which can make you feel sluggish.

Complex carbohydrates are the best foods to power your muscles. They don't leave your body feeling bogged down and tired. That means avoiding heavy usage of red meats and dairy products. These foods throw fats into your blood stream and cut oxygen delivery, along with creating lactic acid build-up that is hard to release from the muscles. If you pedal hard, long days, your quads will become sore and tender to the touch because they can't rid themselves of the excess uric and lactic acid.

Complex carbohydrates include grains, fruits, veggies, beans, pastas, salads, sprouts, whole grain breads and juices. These foods burn cleanly and efficiently, leaving your legs feeling empowered instead of sore. When you're touring in America, it's easy to buy combinations of these items at a grocery deli. Your lunch stop can become a culinary masterpiece!

Nibble Foods

You've only pedaled an hour and you're starving. It's not lunch time, but your stomach needs some food. Voila! Nibble foods. Your handlebar bag is the perfect compartment for carrying trail mix, dried apricots, cashews, or food bars. Use nibble foods to keep energy flowing to your muscles until you stop to raid the main compartment.

You can boil potatoes the night before and use them as tasty nibble foods. Raw carrots make good eating and are easy to keep up front. Rinse them and place them in a plastic bag. Grapes, raisins, cherries and nuts make superb munchies.

Power bars and other granola bars can be munched on as needed.

Additionally, treat yourself by filling your water bottle with a quart of orange juice. Go ahead, it's a hot day. You deserve it.

Who is not a cookie monster? Chocolate-covered graham crackers, Oreos, chocolate chips, cream puffs – they're really bad for you. But who cares? Eat them anyway. Your mother is not around to slap your hand when you raid the cookie jar. (Can you imagine your mother on a touring bike? Dressed in Lycra? What would the neighbors say?) That's the nice thing about being an adult and on tour. You can get away with eating cookies before dinner.

Picking Up Food And Water

Better too early than too late. Keep a close eye on your map around three o'clock in the afternoon. If you see an established campground within your pedaling time, you should prepare for it by buying food within the hour. In summer's prime, you can wait until later as the sun sets around 9 p.m. In Alaska, you can pedal all night in broad daylight!

If it looks like you will be camping in a primitive spot, pick up an extra gallon of water in a collapsible container.

When riding in a mountainous region or where lakes abound, you may want to carry a filter an iodine drops to purify water as needed.

The goal is to be prepared early instead of waiting until the last moment.

Where To Carry Food

Think simple and compact. Packing your panniers is important for both bike stability and food safety on a loaded touring bicycle. The first time you open up a pannier and find strawberry jam dripping out the bottom, it will suddenly occur to you why that pack of honey bees has been escorting you for the past ten miles.

Develop a strategy that fits your style. It will come within a few days on the road. You may have to learn some things the hard way. A few bee stings – or waking up to find your food devoured by raccoons – are the hard ways. The worst (and the most exciting) way is finding a grizzly bear staring at you when you look through your mosquito netting in the morning. Let me tell you, a grizzly has really bad breath!

Place canned foods, boxed foods and other packaged foods in your front panniers. Get rid of any excess packaging by using plastic freezer bags. Use gallon-size freezer bags to ensure nothing leaks.If you have glass containers, make certain they are padded, or transfer the foods to plastic containers.

Bread, eggs, tomatoes, avocados and bananas are big challenges when it comes to avoiding turning them into primordial ooze. It's important that no sugary foods come in contact with your tent. I woke up one night in the Mojave Desert to find ants feeding on the squished bananas that had seeped into the tent fabric. The ants ate through the nylon and were crawling all over the place. It was like one of those Discovery/Nature documentaries on television.

Bread needs to be carried in a cloth netted bag. You can buy them at any department store. Hang the bread off your rear pack via a bungee cord. If it's raining, cover the loaf in plastic. This method also works for bananas. (See Figure 1.)

Tomatoes and peaches are a challenge. Carry them in a plastic container that fits at least two inside and has a lid. You can do the same for avocados. Eggs can be carried six at a time in special plastic egg holders. Buy these at an Army surplus store or other camping outlet. For extra precaution, place eggs at the top of the pannier. There's no sense in having a broken egg slime the entire contents of your pannier.

Apples, oranges and other fruits or vegetables – like potatoes and zucchinis – can be wrapped in cloth or plastic and ride very well at the top of your panniers.

How Much Food To Carry – That Secret Cache

Most human beings worry about running out of food. At home, we stock canned goods that sit for years on the shelf. It's easy to develop that "hoarding" mentality on a bike tour. You're so hungry most of the time, it feels like you might run out of food.

That's why you may choose to carry at least two days' supply of food at all times. It doesn't have to be a heavy addition. Two days means carrying two oatmeal packet, and two rice/lentil dinners. Add a pouch of beef jerky and you're set. Place them at the bottom of your food pack and forget them as dead weight. By carrying those basic carbo/protein foods, you can cruise through any emergency and feel confident at all times that you won't be hungry.

Figure 1.

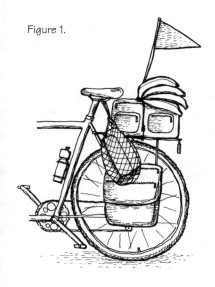

Packing Fragile Foods:

Bananas need special attention. They ripen quickly in the sun and bruise easily on a bumpy road. If you place them in your panniers, they might turn into banana mush. Place them on the top of your rear pack and lock them into place with a bungee cord. The point where the bunch grows together is very strong and will hold with no problems. If it's a rough ride, cushion the bananas with a towel or plastic bag crumpled under them. By using this method, you shouldn't have squashed or bruised bananas. They should last in the sun and heat until you devour them.

Carrying Cooking Gear And The Availability Of Utensils

You normally lean the right side of your bike up against posts and guard rails. That's why you should carry your cooking gear and utensils in the left rear pannier. In that location, you can grab anything when needed. You can make lunch by spreading your tablecloth over the grass and using your stove to heat some tea. Take out your cutting board for cutting meats, cheese, avocado, tomatoes and green peppers. Now, you're ready to pull food from your left front pannier and bread off the rear pack.

As you slice your ham, tomatoes, avocado, green pepper and cucumber, you salivate and your eyes glaze over with ravenous hunger. A layer of mustard on your bread gives your sandwich the perfect flavor accent. It all comes together in a symphony of culinary enchantment.

You made it happen because you protected your food from being turned into multiple layers of sludge, and you had your utensils where you needed them.

Finally, keep your plastic spoon and Swiss Army knife in your handlebar bag. You will use them often, even when you don't have any need to pull out your cooking gear.

Pannier Loading

While on tour, you'll need to keep two panniers in the front loaded with food. Call those panniers your front fuel tanks. On the rear pack, you should use the aforementioned techniques for hauling avocados, eggs, tomatoes, bananas and bread.

It is vitally important to keep your panniers, camping gear and clothing free of liquid sugary foods. Keep all foods sealed. Animals can smell sugar a mile away. If you hear thundering hooves coming toward your tent in the middle of the night, it might be a pack of wild pigs. Yes, it's happened to me. Or worse yet, it could be a bear. The first time you hear a bear grunt outside your tent in the darkness, it will give you a goose bump moment to remember for a lifetime. That is, assuming you live through the night! Do yourself a favor, keep the food in your panniers sealed. Use those freezer bags.

Wiping Up Your Messes

Carry one or two cloth hand towels in a front pannier. Many riders use small canisters of pre-moistened towelettes to wipe hands, silverware, cups and pans. The same thing can be accomplished with hand towels, but you must wash them regularly to kill any germ build-up.

If there's one great thing about being on a bicycle tour, it's enjoying an evening around the campfire with two companions, cooking up a heap of food and talking about the day's ride. The dinner lasts for hours and no one ever admits to being full!

Meals and Deals

"The summer no sweeter was ever;
The sunshiny woods all a thrill;
The grayling asleep in the river,
The big horn sheep on the hill.
The strong life that never knows harness;
The wilds where the caribou call;
The freshness, the freedom, the farness—
O God! How I'm stuck on it all."

Spell of the Yukon by Robert Service, 1890

Food on National Tours

Touring opportunities in North America abound. You can ride through the tropics, deserts, mountains, prairies, tundra and rain forests. You may spend weekends or weeks on tour. A ride across America is the dream of many cyclists.

While on tour in this country, you're near many safety net,including medical assistance and police protection. Your water supply, for the most part, is safe in America and Canada. If in doubt, use a water filter and purification tablets. Many camping stores offer different types of water filters. Check a comparison chart to find one that meets your needs and pocketbook.

On weekend tours, you might want to use easy-to-prepare freeze-dried food packets. They are expensive, but convenient. You will have more time to enjoy the sunset rather than slaving over the hot burner. A fine complement is an already prepared bag of salad from your grocery store. Dessert might be pastry or pudding. Maybe you like wine coolers. Weekend tours can be a fine combination of sight seeing, minimal pedaling and great eating. All you need is one basic dinner; your breakfasts and lunches are easy, and quickly prepared from your food stores. If the route passes deli restaurants or interesting gourmet eateries, by all means, make yourself happy.

On week-long tours, you must plan on daily food procurement and preparation. By using the grocery list and recipes included in this book, you can enjoy your gourmet touring adventure.

It should be noted that simple boxed meals of rice or pasta are offered at reasonable prices in most food stores. You can make yourself happy on macaroni and cheese, rice and lentil pilaf, chop suey dinners and canned stews or tuna, if you choose.

All You Can Eat

For those who love a variety of food and lots of it, stop at a restaurants that feature "All You Can Eat" salad bars. For five bucks, you can eat yourself into hog heaven. My favorite places include Sizzler, Western Sizzlin', Bonanza, Ponderosa, Wendy's, Golden Corral, Soup Plantation and Soup or Salad.

When you roll through a town in the afternoon, stop at this type of restaurants and pig out on 50-item salad bars that often include hot foods too. Chances are you will meet a couple who will be interested in your adventure and invite you over to their house for the night to talk about it.

Church Socials

On weekends, if you ride past a church parking lot with dozens of people walking toward the church, don't hesitate to ask if they're having a dinner social. There is a good chance you can pay a couple of bucks and find yourself in the midst of a potluck extravaganza. Not only that, you will meet some of the finest people in the world.

On one tour in Ontario, Canada, my friends John, Doug and I hit the jackpot. Nothing beats home cooking, and the church folks were happy to have us visit. When we walked in, our eyes grew bigger than dinner plates. On the one side of the church basement was a long table filled with exquisite dishes of every type–roast beef, buttered peas, lasagna, cheese casserole, mashed potatoes in butter, steaming gravies, pork chops, sautéed mushrooms and artichoke hearts, tossed salads, juices, chicken, meat loaf, hot buttered buns and rolls...You get the picture.

On the other side of the room was a 40-foot-long table filled with desserts. I'm not talking about your ordinary display either. This was the "mother lode" of sweet tooth heaven. John nearly fainted from excitement. There were 30 pies of all descriptions, ten dishes of fudge brownies, frozen ice-cream/pudding/custard combinations, chocolate chip cookies with pecans (bury me with one in my mouth), layered German chocolate cakes, lemon cakes, cheesecakes, pudding pies, blueberry muffins, chocolate-covered strawberries, cream-filled eclairs...In other words, we were like kids who had fallen into a cookie jar.

Two hours later, we walked out looking as if we were five months pregnant. John groaned as he patted his stomach, saying, "What kind of death is this? I'm in so much pain, I'm not sure if I want to die, or go back in there and eat some more."

Budget Tours

Some riders may be financially challenged. Every corner cut is a dollar saved. A few cyclists travel without a tent, while others wear old shoes. They roll into campgrounds after the ranger has left the collection booth, and they vanish onto the highway before sunrise—to avoid paying a camping fee.

Some brag about living on $5 a day for food.

You may be in that category. It's very difficult to live on $5 a day in the United State, but it may be possible if you don't mind a limited food selection. The key: The food you eat must be nutritious to power you down the road.

If you're on a tight budget, center your diet on pastas, grains and root vegetables with legumes for protein and carbohydrates. You will not be a "Gourmet Touring Bicyclist, " but you will maintain the strength and energy to pedal another day.

Not only that, you will be able to brag to your friends ten years later about how you suffered on your pilgrimage across America by eating potatoes, rice and noodles for 90 days in a row. They, of course, will at that point realize why they suspected you were crazed in the head all those years.

To save money and meet a $5 to $7 daily food budget, you must be very basic in your food intake. It leaves little room for the imagination or your palette's enjoyment.

Budget Meal Selections

Breakfast:
Regular oatmeal cooked in water. Bag of raisins or brown sugar to sweeten. Apple or orange to top it off. Stuff yourself.

My grandma used to say, "Oatmeal will stick to your ribs 'til noon." It sure will, and it's a cheap way to fire your boilers. Your mother may think you're crazed for riding a bicycle on tour, but listen to your grandmother.

Lunch:
Several large boiled potatoes left over from the night before. Really cheap and nutritious and filling. Peanut butter and jam sandwich with bananas sliced in. Carrots and other vegetables. A banana or other fruit.

Dinner:
Boiled noodles and broth or boiled rice and lentils or potatoes. Carrots, zucchini, onions and tomatoes. Possibly cut strips of jerky into the entree.

Optional:
Carry a mousetrap and catch a mouse – good protein. Make sure it's a gray one because the black ones taste awful.

Vitamins

While on tour, you'll burn huge amounts of energy and place increased stresses on your body. If you're eating on a budget, you may not receive all the vitamins and minerals needed to resupply your body. To cover that possibility, carry a supply of vitamin and mineral supplements. That way, you're covered, and it's inexpensive.

A touring rider of any age expends enormous amounts of energy. That energy releases "free radicals," which break down body tissue. By maintaining proper vitamin and mineral intake through supplements, your body can neutralize the effects of those rascals.

Other Ways To Save Money

Finally, save money on food purchases by stopping at farmer's markets, and day-old bread outlets.

I met a guy standing on a San Francisco street corner with his raggedy touring bike and a sign on his chest, looking as forlorn as he could possibly manage. It read, "Homeless bicycle rider. Will bicycle for food. God Bless You."

As my Deore XT derailleur is my witness, I saw several people drop money into his helmet!

Food On International Tours

Eating Out

A good friend of mine toured Africa for 16 months. It took only one sandwich from a street vendor to give him stomach worms. You may reduce your chances of ingesting parasites by avoiding buying foods from vendors. They may not understand food sanitation and consequently prepare their foods in unsanitary conditions. You will avoid the consequences by preparing and eating your own foods.

However, if you do eat meals prepared by others, make sure the food (soups and main dishes) are hot when you receive them. You need to be somewhat confident that cooked foods are reasonably safe. In places like Africa, you court danger if you eat sandwiches and other uncooked foods prepared by foreign hands.

If sickness visits your bowels, you must endure it. As long as it doesn't kill you, it'll make you tougher. On the sickest day of my life, riding over a 15,000-foot pass out of Bolivia in the Andes, I watched two condors fly down from 18,000 feet to investigate me. When they leveled off about 30 feet from my handlebars, I couldn't tell whether they were going to eat me, or were just wondering whether or not I was invading their air space It was one heck of a magical moment, seeing those 12 foot wing-spanned birds up close. Seconds later, they powered back to 18,000 feet and out of my life. Even though I was sick as a dog, it was one of the high points of the tour.

Usually, after becoming miserably sick once, your body will adjust to the foods and bacteria and be fine.

Other Food Considerations

Often, milk is not safe and not pasteurized. It will be presented and sold in open bottles at room temperature. Meat, also, is presented at room temperature on dirty cutting blocks with flies crawling all over it. Your appetite implodes. At about that moment you scream, "I need a Big Mac, McFries, Chicken McNuggets, McAnything that won't kill me!"

What can you do to avoid food poisoning? Wash all your food. Peel all fruits. Avoid keeping leftovers. Unless you kill the chicken yourself, or butcher the cow, or catch the fish, stay away from hazardous flesh.

Instead, stick to veggies, pastas, grains, fruits that you peel, breads and crackers. Cook foods yourself. That gives you power over your own health. With any luck, you'll travel through areas at harvest time where you can purchase foods easily or even find them in abundance for free.

During a ride from Santiago to Puerto Montt, Chile, we pedaled through 800 miles of wild blackberries, which grew along the road and were at the height of the season. Our hands, mouths and teeth were deliciously blue the whole time.

No matter where you pedal in the world, you are sure to find basic foods: oatmeal, grains, potatoes, corn, peas, squash, onions, tomatoes, fruits of all kinds, breads and spices. These basic foods can be incorporated into your diet.

However, I must tell you what was told to me around a campfire in Brazil. I met up with a fellow named Gary who was on a three-year bicycle tour around the world. I can not vouch for his credibility, but he had endured some amazing culinary experiences.

He warned, "Mark my words, young man. It's dangerous around here. If you get invited into some local cannibal tribe's dinner gathering, you might be served human brains. As God is my witness, I'm telling you, don't eat 'em! They usually throw the brains to the dogs and women. Often times, the dogs thrive on them. But the women come down with a gender-based predicament that makes them laugh themselves to death."

"You've got to be kidding me," I said, incredulously. "I've never heard of anything like that."

"No, I'm not kiddin'," he said. "Not only that, you better be careful of a biting butterfly in these parts called a Macho. It looks like a peanut with huge wings. If that little bugger bites you, it means you better have sexual intercourse within 24 hours or you will face certain, agonizing death."

"Thanks," I said, not knowing if he was living in some other zone that I wasn't aware of at that point in my life.

Good Foods

After you have prepared yourself for the difficulties in Third World countries, the key thought is—enjoy yourself. There are many gourmet delights in restaurants around the world. In the Galapagos Islands, you'll be dining at the village cafe in Santa Cruz while porpoises jump through the surf. In Kathmandu, Nepal, gorge yourself on dahl-bott, a rice/potato/bean dish that tastes better than your mom's best roast beef dinner. Mount Everest's shadow may play on your shoulders. In Brazil, you can't help enjoy the finest in exotic fruit dishes after a sumptuous meal. On the beach the folks in string bikinis offer a second kind of dessert...visual! Finally, eat a fish dish in Bari, Italy, on the waterfront with the round table, red/white-checkered table cloth and three violinists serenading you and your lady.

Grocery List and Recipes

"By now, a million pedal strokes have etched the muscles in my legs with a single purpose: to power the cranks and move the bicycle forward. Food flows into my body, bringing it power and strength. It is no longer a question of struggle. Now the journey evolves into the spiritual realm – where the pedaling is instinctive. It's a free-flow energy that comes through my body and willingly expresses itself in the flight of the pedals."
The Gourmet Bicyclist riding over a 15,500-foot pass in Bolivia, 1988

When you go into the store, it's a good idea to know what you want to buy for the evening meal. Otherwise, you may end up with too much food or not enough. Take a list with you to make sure you purchase everything you need to cook dinner, breakfast and lunch for the next day, plus nibble foods. Keep a tab on what you have used, in order to replenish. Buy quantities that you intend to use or carry. Many times you can pick up small packets of ketchup, mustard, mayonnaise and hot sauce at a deli for free.

Check your spice bottle to make sure you have enough of what you need.

Look for foods rumbling around in the bottom of your panniers. Use them up before duplicate buying occurs. Use this list as a prompter only.

Grocery List

1. Bread, bagels, tortillas, crackers
2. Fruits – apples, bananas, plums, nectarines, pears, tomatoes, oranges, grapefruits, cherries, grapes, prunes, berries, etc.
3. Veggies – potatoes, zucchini, onion, green pepper, red pepper, carrots, mushrooms, cucumbers, lettuce, spinach, broccoli, cauliflower, Brussels sprouts, avocados, squashes, alfalfa sprouts, etc.
4. Grains – rice, barley, wheat, oats, couscous, etc.
5. Legumes – lentils, red beans, lima beans etc.
6. Power Bars/granola bars
7. Nuts
8. Peanut butter/almond butter
9. Jam/Jelly
10. Trail mix
11. Seasonings
12. Salt/pepper, chili powder/sauce

13. Butter/margarine/cream cheese
14. Cooking oil
15. Soy sauce/mustard
16. Soups (instant packs)
17. Your favorite instant coffee
18. Tea
19. Hot chocolate
20. Orange/fruit juices
21. Spaghetti/pasta
22. Rice/pilaf
23. Spaghetti sauce
24. Lentil/pilaf
25. Brown sugar
26. Raisins
27. Oatmeal/cereal/grits
28. Cookies and more cookies
29. Sugar
30. Canned foods:
    Beef stew
    Corned beef hash
    Chili stew
    Pork and beans
    Tuna/crab
31. Dairy and Meat:
    Cheese
    Milk
    Yogurt
    Ham and turkey slices
    Meat of all types: bacon, sausage, chicken
32. At the deli:
    Macaroni salad
    Potato salad
    Jell-o/puddings
    Fruit salad
    Cole slaw
    Tacos, beef and veggie
    Egg rolls
33. Write in your particular needs:
    Popcorn
    White wine
    Oregano
    Marjoram
    Falafel mix

Recipes

The following combinations are easy to prepare and tasty for breakfast, lunch and dinner. You may add to your repertoire as you become more creative while on tour. Further, you might meet someone who has developed his or her own gourmet meals. Ask to borrow the recipes.

I have found that the end of the day brings a pleasant exhaustion. I'm hungry and tired. I want my dinners to be easy. I don't want to jump through a bunch of hoops to prepare my food.

These recipes are noted as to whether they are vegetarian or meat-based. Some are interchangeable. Choose which works best for you. The recipes serve one except where noted. Double the recipes if you need more.

The operative words are simple and fast. You're hungry. Let's eat!

Breakfast

Cold "Crank Arm" Cereal

(Easy. Vegetarian.)

Ingredients:
Cold cereal – Grapenuts, Cheerios, granola
Milk (powdered), orange juice or water. You might be able to use fresh
  milk if you keep it in a cold stream or lake.
Raisins
Sliced bananas

How to prepare:
  Heat water for tea or coffee first. Cut up fruits and add to cereal. Pour milk, juice or water on cereal. Serve with bread spread with peanut butter and jelly, tea, coffee or hot chocolate and an apple, orange or nectarine.

Hot, Steamy And Tasty "Stick To Your Ribs" Oatmeal

(Takes longer to prepare. Vegetarian.)

Ingredients:
1 cup water
½ cup oatmeal, regular or instant
Raisins or dried cherries
Sliced peaches, nectarines, apple
Cashews
Maple syrup

How to prepare:
  Boil water for coffee or hot chocolate first. Boil 1 cup water, add oatmeal, simmer until cooked. Cut up fruits on cutting board and mix into oatmeal. Add raisins to cooking oatmeal. Keep an eye on oatmeal so it

doesn't burn. Take off heat, add fruits, nuts and maple syrup. Serve with whole wheat bread spread with peanut butter and jelly and tea, coffee or hot chocolate.

Mouth-Watering "Top Tube" Yogurt Treat

(Vegetarian.)

Ingredients:
Muesli cereal, multi-grain with nuts, dates
Sliced pears
Cashews or other nuts
Sliced apples
Yogurt, vanilla or plain (6 oz., 8 oz., 12 oz.)
Milk (pint or a quart)

How to prepare:
Boil water for coffee, tea or hot chocolate first. Cut up fruits and add to cereal. Use your cooking pot to mix yogurt/milk into cereal. Serve with tea, hot chocolate or coffee.

Scramlett "Tandem" Omelet

(Serves one or two persons. Meat-based. Ovo-vegetarians may omit meat from this menu.)

Ingredients:
Three to four eggs
Oil or butter
Green/red peppers, chopped
Salt and pepper
Mushrooms, chopped
Last night's boiled potato, diced
Small onion, diced
Two slices cheese (cheddar/ Swiss/Muenster)
Diced ham (even Spam!) or beef jerky, chopped
Tomato, chopped

How to prepare:
Prepare your stove, cooking area. Heat water for coffee or tea. Cut up food as required. Heat and oil pan. Sauté diced ham or jerky first. Remove meat from pan. Scramble eggs and pour into pan. Cook until set, then add veggies and meat. Fold eggs over to form Scramlett, spice as needed. Add cheese to top of Scramlett.

Banana Or Strawberry "Pannier" Pancakes

(Vegetarian.)

Ingredients:
Complete pre-packaged pancake mix
Water or milk for pancake mix
Fresh or frozen strawberries
Bananas
Butter
Syrup/jam/peanut butter
Oil

How to prepare:
Heat oil in pan. Prepare pancake mix according to instructions. Add two tablespoons of oil to pancake batter. Cut up bananas into round slices. Pour batter into pan. Place five slices of bananas into cooking pancake. Turn over and finish cooking. Serve with strawberries, butter, syrup or jam.

Frosty's Hashbrowned "Broken Spoke" Extravaganza

(Vegetarian or meat-based.)

Ingredients:
Frozen hashbrowns from your favorite grocery store
Pepper and salt
¼ cup dry powdered milk
One small onion, chopped
Two eggs
Hot water
Oil
Green/red peppers, chopped
Two slices cheddar cheese
Ground beef or diced ham
Bagels and cream cheese

How to prepare:
Prepare stove, pan and oil. Cook ground beef or diced ham first. Drain off oil – set meat aside in extra pan. Place thawed hashbrowns and onions and peppers into pan. Scramble the eggs right into the hashbrowns as they near completion. Add ground beef or diced ham. Season with spices and add powdered milk. Cut cheese slices over hashbrowns. Compliment with bagel and top off with fresh apple.

Tasty "Top Tube" Tuna Scramlett

(Meat-based.)

Ingredients:
1 can of tuna
2 eggs (four eggs for two servings)
Pinch of salt
Pinch of dill weed
2 tablespoons milk
4 slices of your favorite cheese

How to prepare:
 Beat the eggs with salt, dill weed and milk. Cook eggs. When nearly set, add tuna. Add cheese, cover until melted.

LUNCH

Prepared on the ground, on a picnic table, on a bridge, or on the back of your bike pack, lunch while touring becomes a high point of the day. You may choose magnificent views across rugged canyons where hawks soar on the updrafts. Or, you might find a quiet spot deep in a forest. Rivers and waterfalls make excellent backdrops. That's the joy of bicycle touring, you choose what's best for you.

You may find you have some sandwich fixings left over. For instance, you may not use an entire sliced tomato on your Avocado Caliper Sandwich. Don't fret the leftovers – eat them!

Avocado "Caliper" Sandwich

(Brake for this one! Vegetarian or meat-based.)

Ingredients:
Wheat bread or pita bread
Green pepper, sliced
Avocado, sliced
Tomato, sliced
Cucumber, sliced
Ham, sliced
Mustard
Banana, apple, orange

How to prepare:
 Prepare avocado, tomato, cucumber, green pepper. Squirt mustard on bread. Spread avocado onto bread. Layer on tomato, cucumber, green pepper. Accompany with fruit.

"Brake Pad" Cheese Sandwich Special

(Vegetarian or meat-based.)

Ingredients:
Whole wheat bread
Any type of cheese, sliced
Red pepper, sliced
Slices of ham (or cooked chicken from deli)
Tomato, sliced
Sprouts
Mustard
Orange, kiwi, nectarine

How to prepare:
Cut it all up and slap it down. Open your mouth wide. Accompany with fruit.

The "Freewheel" Banana-Peanut Butter-And-Jam Sandwich

(Vegetarian, unless you want to add pork chops to the peanut butter!)

Ingredients:
Bread
Peanut butter
Jam
Banana
Watermelon

How to prepare:
If you don't know how to make a PB and J, go back to third grade. Slice round circles of banana and stick into the peanut butter. Slurp down with a juicy watermelon.

The "Bottom Bracket" Soup And Sandwich Lunch Special

(For cold days. Vegetarian or meat-based.)

Ingredients:
Your favorite soup out of a can or packet, veggie or meat-based
Any of your favorite sandwich fixings
Half a loaf of bread
Yogurt with cut-up fruit

How to prepare:
Take out your cook stove and light. Place pan over flame and add water as instructed in soup directions. Pour in soup from packet or can and cook. Dunk bread into broth and enjoy. Finish off with a fruit and yogurt dessert. Save a couple of slices of bread to make your favorite sandwich, and eat with the soup.

Cold "Chain Stay" Burrito Sandwich

(Vegetarian or meat-based.)

Ingredients:
Refried beans
Tomatoes
Thinly sliced cheese
Sliced black olives
Chunky salsa (small jar as it doesn't keep for long)
Sprouts or lettuce
Jerky or diced ham
Tortilla shells

How to prepare:
Spread refried beans on tortilla shell. Dice tomatoes and add to beans. Place cheese, olives, meat, sprouts and lettuce on top. Add salsa to suit. Roll into burrito.

"Touring Triple" Tuna Sandwich

(Meat-based.)

Ingredients:
1 can of tuna
Mayonnaise
Onion powder
Wheat bread
Sprouts
Muenster or provolone cheese
Dill pickle
Celery

How to prepare:
Mix mayo and onion powder with tuna. Spread on bread. Layer on cheese, sliced pickle. Voilá, a taste sensation. Serve the celery on the side.

Reuben "Rim" Sandwich

(Vegetarian.)

Ingredients:
Rye bread
Mayonnaise
Dijon mustard
Swiss cheese
Sprouts
Pickle

How to prepare:
Spread mayo and mustard on bread. Layer on cheese and sprouts. Add sliced pickle.

DINNERS

By candle lantern or brilliant sunset sky.

Endorphin Salad Special

(Get "high" on this one! Vegetarian.)

Compliment your dinners by buying a head of lettuce and some salad veggies to go along with it. Keep a couple of juicy tomatoes for topping it all off. In America, you might enjoy the quick-and-easy convenience of an "already prepared" salad. Buy a two-pound bag of salad greens along with dressing at any grocery store. It's quick and easy, plus there's no waste from buying too much.

"Chain Whip" Pasta Casserole

(Vegetarian or meat-based.)

Ingredients:
4 cups of water
1 teaspoon salt
Chopped carrots, zucchini, onions
¼ cube of butter
¼ cup of flour for thickening
2 to 3 cups pasta
½ cup milk or powdered milk mixed with ½ cup water
Your favorite meat (for T-Rex cyclists!)

How to prepare:
Boil water and add veggies. Add pasta, spices. Keep stirring so as not to burn for 15 to 20 minutes. When pasta is cooked, remove from heat. Add meat with butter. Mix milk and flour in bowl and stir to smooth sauce. Add pasta to sauce. Enjoy.

With this basic casserole recipe, you may add chicken, fish, beef, pork. Keep using the basic plan and you can enjoy easy diversity.

"Broken Spokes" Spaghetti Spectacle

(Vegetarian or meat-based.)

Ingredients:
Spaghetti noodles
6 cups of water
Prepared pasta sauce (any brand you like)
Broccoli and cauliflower
Salt
Ground beef
Bread, bagels, rolls
Water for coffee, tea, hot chocolate

How to prepare:

Boil water for coffee, tea or hot chocolate first. Brown hamburger, drain grease. Boil six cups of water and add spaghetti. Add salt if desired. When spaghetti is cooked, drain and set off to side. Pour sauce into pan. Cut up broccoli and cauliflower and add to sauce, with the meat, if desired. Let simmer until cooked. If you have a friend, one portion of the meal could be cooked at same time on his or her burner. Pour sauce over spaghetti. Sop up sauce with bread.

"Flat Tire" Rice Delight

(No pump needed. Vegetarian or meat-based.)

Ingredients:
Rice (a box of Near East or Rice a Roni with spice packet)
Soft tortilla shells
Lentils, pilaf
Ground beef
Coffee, tea, hot chocolate

How to prepare:

Boil water for tea, coffee, hot chocolate first. Brown ground beef, set aside. Boil water and add rice and lentils, spice packet. Cook for about 30 minutes. When done, lay tortilla shells out. Put meat in shell. Pour in rice and fold to encase inside the shell. Eat like a sandwich.

The "Chain Ring" Couscous Crunch

(Fastest hot food you can get down your gullet! Vegetarian or meat-based.)

Ingredients:
1 box of instant couscous (from Near East or Fantastic Foods, available in most grocery stores)
1¾ cups water
1 bag of frozen veggies, thawed
Ham or ground beef (for meat lovers)

How to prepare:

Boil water. Add couscous and spice packet. Five minutes later, take off heat and let stand. Cook meat as desired. Heat veggies in boiling water. Serve as a side dish to couscous.

The "Head Set" Hamburger

(For T-Rex cyclists with a romantic flare! Meat-based.)

Ingredients:
Ground beef
Bread
Tomato
Small onion
Cheese slices
Ketchup
Coffee, cigarettes and a bottle of gin
Girlfriend taking a bath in the lake
Warm summer night with no mosquitoes (yeah, right)
Something flying around the campsite
Full moon

How to prepare:
Have cigarette dangling from your mouth like James Dean. Keep a jigger of gin off to the side, along with wine. Remember that cork screw on your Swiss Army knife? Get ready to pull the cork because she just stepped out of the lake and...the only thing she's wearing is silver moonlight...

Boil water for black coffee, but don't dump it on yourself. Make ground beef into patties if you're not too nervous. Cut up tomato and onion, but don't cut your fingers off in your excitement.

She's moving toward you with that look on her face. Oops, that little winged peanut just bit you and her...Your appetite for food just died. You've caught the disease of the dreaded Macho. Forget hamburgers, extinguish cigarette, quickly throw a shot of gin to the back of your mouth. Brush your teeth. She's closing in on you. There's no escape. You only have 24 hours to live unless you...

Hot Chili Over The "Dropouts"

(Vegetarian.)

Ingredients:
4 cups of water
1 cup of lentils
Three-ounce can of tomato paste
One small onion, chopped
1 tablespoon of chili powder
1 tablespoon of oregano
1 teaspoon of garlic powder (Don't plan on kissing your girlfriend after
    dinner)
Slab of your favorite cheese

How to prepare:
Combine everything, except cheese, in pan. Cook on simmer for 35 to 40 minutes. Serve topped with cheese.

Hot "Pedal Faster" Potato Soup

(Vegetarian.)

Ingredients:
Two potatoes, chopped
1 cup of milk, or a half-cup of powdered milk mixed with water
¼ cup of flour
One small onion, chopped
½ cup water
Dash of salt/pepper
Slash of oil
Your favorite cheese
Bread

How to prepare:

Place all ingredients into a pot and bring to a boil. Keep stirring until it develops a soft texture. Place bread in extra pan. Pour soup over bread. Cut the cheese onto the top and let melt.

Sally's "Saddle Sore" Tortillas

(Vegetarian.)

Ingredients:
Four tortilla shells
½ cup of rice
1½ cup water
1 teaspoon salt
Dash of cumin
Dash of cilantro
3 pats of butter
Optional: Peppers, canned black beans, hot sauce, butter

How to prepare:

In a covered pot, boil water with rice for 20 minutes until water is absorbed. Add chopped peppers, cilantro, cumin and butter to rice, stir. Rinse black beans. Add beans and rice to tortilla, spice with hot sauce.

Falafel "Fork And Frame" Burgers

(Vegetarian.)
Hamburger buns or wheat bread
Falafel mix (available in the health food section of most grocery stores)
Water
Safflower oil
Veggies (carrots, tomatoes, cucumbers)
Garlic

How to prepare:

Mix falafel mix with water according to package directions, add garlic and bring to consistency to make a patty. Heat pan and add safflower oil.

Cook patties. Cut veggies. When patties are cooked, layer with veggies on buns or break to make sandwich.

Pedaler's Pilaf With Steamed Cauliflower Au Gratin

(Vegetarian.)

Ingredients:
½ cup brown rice
½ cup lentils
1 fistful of peanuts
1 fistful of raisins
1 white or yellow onion, diced
1 or 2 potatoes (optional)
1½ to 1¾ cups water (more at high altitude)
1 tablespoon curry powder
½ cauliflower, chopped
Grated Parmesan cheese

How to prepare:
   Place rice, lentils, water, peanuts, raisins in a pot. Cover with water and bring to a boil. Stir in onion, lower heat. After five minutes, stir in potatoes. When water level drops below level of mixture, lay cauliflower on top and cover pot again. When all the water has boiled away, remove from the flame and sprinkle cheese on cauliflower. Voilá, a two-course meal in one pot!

Chicken "Tandem" With Tang

(Fowl-based.)

Ingredients:
2 chicken breasts
Half a stick of butter
2 nectarines, peeled, pitted and cut into quarters
2 tablespoons flour
Salt/pepper
1 cup whipping cream

How to prepare:
   Cook chicken in butter on your stove, or on stick over campfire (sauté in pan with butter after chicken is cooked). Add nectarines and continue to sauté for 10 minutes. Keep chicken and nectarines warm by fire.
   Sauce: Add flour to the pan drippings and mix thoroughly using your plastic fork. Add cream and continue stirring over heat until sauce thickens. Add salt and pepper. Pour over chicken and nectarines. Enjoy.

"Cotterless Crank" Carrot Soup

(Vegetarian.)

Ingredients:
⅓ cup butter
½ cup chopped onion
2 cups sliced carrots
½ cup long grain or wild rice
3 cups of chicken stock or 3 chicken bouillon cubes in 3 cups of water
2 cups milk
Butter
½ teaspoon curry powder
¼ teaspoon salt

How to prepare:

In a large pot, sauté onions in butter. Add rice and carrots and stir until coated. Add curry and chicken stock. Simmer until carrots are tender and rice is cooked. Salt to taste. Add milk and simmer to desired taste.

Baked Potato "Fond Of You" Delight

(Vegetarian.)

Ingredients:
1 onion
1 garlic clove
1 eight-ounce can of cut-up tomatoes
¼ teaspoon of oregano
½ teaspoon basil
8 ounces cheddar cheese, sliced or diced
1 ounce Parmesan cheese, sliced or diced
2 cooked potatoes (baked in tin foil or boiled)
Safflower oil

How to prepare:

Either bake the potato, wrapped in tin foil, in the campfire, or boil it until done. In pan, sauté chopped onion and garlic. Add chopped tomatoes, basil, oregano. Simmer. Add cheddar and Parmesan, stir until smooth. Cut open potatoes and pour sauce over.

"Pedaling" Pork Chops And Rice

(Meat-based.)

Ingredients:
1 or 2 pork chops
1½ teaspoons oil
½ cup beef broth
2 tablespoons dry white wine
½ small onion, chopped
4 carrots, sliced lengthwise
¼ cup quick rice
Dash of oregano
Dash of salt and pepper
Dash of marjoram

How to prepare:
Cook chops in pan until well browned (may be done over the camp-fire). Remove from heat and put aside. Drain grease from pan. Add broth, wine, carrot, onion and seasonings to pan and bring to boil. Stir in rice. Boil until all the liquid is gone. Add chops to your dish.

Special Note For Fishermen:

If you bring your rod and tackle on your tour, no doubt a trout or salmon will land on your dinner table at some point. The key, after cleaning your fish, is to prepare it so it retains its fresh flavor. The easiest way to cook fresh fish is to wrap it, some butter and a little water in aluminum foil, seal the package, and poach over an open flame. You can add onion or garlic to the pouch if you choose.

You also can pan-fry the fish in bacon grease or butter on your stove. Either method will render a succulent entree.

Desserts

Desserts are a personal taste item. You can buy ice cream, puddings, fruits, yogurts and cookies at any store. I try to keep my desserts limited to fruits. You will discover your own style.

Sometimes You Have To Go Without A Mirror To See Yourself

"No diet will remove all the fat from your body because the brain is entirely fat. Without the brain, you might look good, but all you could do is run for public office."
Covert Bailey

When a bicycle adventure stretches into weeks, months – even years – profound changes in the cyclist occur. New perspectives arise that seldom emerge in daily routine existence.

Basic living dominates. I wake up with the birds at dawn. Hunger pulls at my stomach and a hearty breakfast fills me with energy. Later, having washed dishes, I take a bath in the lake near my camp. I stretch my muscles. That done, I stuff the panniers and break camp. Each piece of equipment has a specific place on my bike's frame. Everything is simple, straightforward, black and white.

What time is it? The present. What day is it? Today. Where am I? On the planet Earth. What's in the news? Good question. Stress? What's that? Anything new in my life? Every mile. Positive expectations? Moment to moment.

If I'm with a pedal partner, our conversation runs the length and breadth of the globe. We talk about life – the meaning or non-meaning of it – along with the futility, frustration and turmoil in the world. At the other end of the scale, we talk about people and places. We are grateful for our fortunate circumstances. What's up ahead is a favorite topic because it holds expectations. If it's mountains, we know clear streams will be our constant companions on climbs and descents. Something about moving water makes pedaling up a mountain grade seem effortless. Along the route, we know lakes and abundant wildlife await us

One important aspect of traveling with a partner is the emotional bonding that takes place. I know what love feels like when I've toured with someone. I've fallen in love with my best friends on our adventures. My female friends have shared wonderful campfires under starlit skies, swum in turquoise pools, watched desert sunrises and climbed over ledges to see the world from behind waterfalls.

When I'm alone, I talk to myself. The solitary times make me appreciate moments of fellowship. My whole day is brightened when someone stops to talk along the highway or in a campsite. I'm as interested in their journey as they are in mine. Travelers enjoy a different mindset – their spirits exude optimism through discovery. Sharing it creates a mutual high.

The one thing I notice as weeks turn into months is that I'm less concerned with things that don't affect me. Every day flows naturally into new people, sights and perspectives. A deep peacefulness pervades my demeanor. I used to wonder what happened to bring on that peacefulness, and one day I figured it out.

Do you know most people look into the mirror every day of their lives? When they do, they become critical of themselves. They aren't pretty or handsome enough. They focus on minor flaws. They might not like their nose shape, eye color or lips. They compare themselves to someone else. It's an endless cycle of self-denigration. Youth slips away each day, and their minds argue against it. The mirror reflects their personal insecurities. It focuses them on themselves instead of on the quality of their lives. You can't see depth of character or caliber of personality in a mirror. It's the one aspect of a human being that presents itself through daily interaction with others.

Perhaps looking in a mirror determines self-esteem, whether high or low. That's unfortunate, because we are what we are. No two are the same, everyone is unique. When I was a kid, my brother possessed golden boy good looks. Girls fell over themselves when he walked by. I never quite measured up, no matter how many times I combed my hair. I compared myself to my brother, and later, to celebrities. No way could I be that handsome, and no way could women look as beautiful as the stars on the silver screen. Yet, I had been measuring myself against others and ignoring my own qualities.

One day, my friend Mike told me he was tired of me berating myself. He told me that I had one of the greatest assets he had ever seen in a person.

''What is it?'' I asked. ''Will it make me money?''

''Don't you get it?'' he answered. ''You have the greatest gift I've ever seen.''

"What good is it doing me? Why can't I see it?" I asked again.

"It's your enthusiasm," he answered. "You can't create it, or buy it. You have it in spades, and it's going to be with you all your life. It's your gift to others, the joy of being alive."

I have never complained since. Thanks, Mike.

Ever wonder why those handsome and beautiful movie stars have such tragic personal lives? They marry among themselves on physical attraction. Their spiritual, emotional and personal selves get lost in the hype. Do they share common interests? Do they have similar backgrounds? Did they take time to become friends? One day, they both have to get down to daily living together. If either enlaces a balanced self-concept, or they don't have interests in common, the relationship is doomed. No matter how good looking someone is, it's the character that expresses itself to the world each day.

On a spring tour, my friend Paul complained that he wasn't as good looking as "those other guys." He lamented not being tall enough. He bemoaned his skinny build. Yet, in reality, Paul is good-looking, well-built and quite dashing. He possesses average height, but I never considered height a measure of his humanity. I told him that I was tired of his maligning himself, and asked him to say positive things or nothing at all. I asked Paul if he would like to give up his full head of hair for another man's six feet of height, but sparse hair? If he were taller, better looking, or perfectly built, would he have more women? Would our friendship become better? I told him it wouldn't matter to me if he were the ugliest person on earth. Some of the most physically beautiful people in the world are the ugliest, saddest and most loathsome. I told him that character reaches beyond looks. It reaches deeper levels of being that have nothing to do with the physical world. Character is not a comparison or judgment. It's an acceptance of yourself and your feelings for your friends.

A short time later, Paul came up to me with a big smile on his face.

"What's up?" I asked.

"You know that talk we had a few months ago about accepting myself?"

"Sure."

"You know something, I've been taking stock of my life," he said. "I've got a good job, a great girlfriend, a nice house, sports and good friends. What you said has finally gotten through to my brain. I like myself."

"Great," I said, smiling. "You know, you have to take inventory once in a while to realize how good your life is."

"Thanks," he said.

"Thank Mike," I answered, thinking back to the old friend who had helped me deal with the same issues.

In the end, I'm convinced that friends walk into one another's lives to help each other out. They offer support during rough times, and enhance the joy of the good times. They make a day on the road, snow, or water, or at dinner or the movies a time of celebration.

What if someone you know lies or plays unfairly? What if their dishonesty angers you, whether it be a public figure or a personal friend? They obviously look into a mirror too much, but can't see themselves. In the end, dishonest people sink to a level with others like themselves, or no one at all. Their prison is a lack of human interaction based on respect. I never feel angry at dishonest people, because I know they pay the ultimate price—no self-esteem and loss of quality friends. I can't think of a worse fate.

On a bicycle adventure, I rarely look into a mirror to see myself. Soon, I forget about what I look like. I'm just me. Doug is himself. Pam bubbles with her usual excitement. Bryan talks his head off. Susie glories in living. John laughs at the wind. Paul cracks jokes. Linda loves sunshine. Phil sings in the saddle. Laura glows with enthusiasm. My friends and I go along without worrying about our clothes, how we look, what we do for a living, or what the Joneses have. We accept ourselves and each other with no conditions. The moment is the only thing that is important. Participating in that moment means we're not looking at reflections of ourselves – rather, we are living. In that participation comes unconditional self-acceptance.

Samuel Johnson said: "The fountain of content must spring up in the mind, and they who hath so little knowledge of human nature as to seek happiness by changing anything but their own disposition, will waste their lives in fruitless efforts and multiply the grief they propose to remove."

Sometimes you have to go without a mirror to see yourself.

Part Three
Appendices

Suppliers and Touring Companies

"You've been so long in the rain, you feel like a dirty dish rag. But despite the misery of your soaked body, you look around to see verdant leaves dripping with water. The air enters your nostrils vibrantly clean. To experience adventure, you must be willing to be uncomfortable at times and enjoy loneliness by being happy with your own singing. A song pops out of your mouth…"It rained all night the day I left, the weather it was fine…"

The Gourmet Bicyclist in the rain forest of Washington state, 1989

Quality Camping Stores, Bicycle Outfitters And National/International Touring Companies

Touring bicyclists are a special breed of individuals. It takes muscle and guts to pedal down the highway. Mountains test your gumption and deserts test your will. It's tough out there. Your character is challenged every day, and your inner being is affected by the hardships and joys you experience while pedaling your bike.

There is something special about your mode of travel. It creates magical moments that can not be generated any other way. You're riding a thin line between personal power and physical exhaustion. Those enchanting moments just happen. You can't look for them, nor can you expect them. You enter into them through the forces of Nature that swirl around you.

The key to enjoying the charm is having the best equipment you can afford. The following organizations base their research and development on making camping and bicycling better for you. They guarantee their products. I have used gear from all of them. I have never been disappointed, and if I was, I was given a replacement or refund for my concerns.

By calling their 800 numbers, you can receive a catalog with all the equipment you may need:

Quality Camping Stores/Bicycle Outfitters

Performance: Primarily bicycles, clothing, gloves, helmets, tents, shoes, panniers, rain gear. Excellent quality and excellent warranty. Catalog. Call: 1-800-727-2453.

Bike Nashbar: Bicycle clothing, bicycles, everything you need. Excellent quality, guarantee and service. Catalog. Call: 1-800-627-4227.

Diamond Brand Tents: Some of the best tents for the lowest cost in the United States. I use the Acorn, a half-dome. Regardless of the brand of tent you purchase, make sure it has a vestibule. These come in handy for storing gear during a rainstorm. Call: 1-800-459-6262.

The North Face: Top-quality gear – a little pricey, but with an excellent guarantee. Tents, sleeping bags, cooking gear, air mattresses. Catalog. Call: 1-800-447-2333.

Campmor: Outstanding camping store. Guarantee. Many items and latest equipment innovations. Catalog. Write: P.O. Box 700-04, Saddle River, NJ 07458. Call: 1-800-230-2151.

Madden Mountaineering: Some of the best panniers made. New waterproof panniers coming out in summer, 1996. Well-designed. Excellent quality. Outstanding day packs. Catalog. Write: 2400 Central Ave., Boulder, CO 80304.

REI: Top-quality camping and bicycle equipment store. REI features a stove comparison chart second to none. The store carries Ortlieb panniers, which are totally waterproof. Catalog. Write: 1700 45th St. East, Sumner, WA 98390. Call: 1-800-426-4840.

Eastern Mountain Sports: Excellent camping gear. Good service. Guarantee. Write: Vose Farm Road, Peterborough, NH 03458.

Cannondale: Excellent bike manufacturer. Excellent clothing products. Bike trailers if you want to bring a child along on a tour. Write: 35 Pulaski St., Stamford, CT 06902.

Early Winters: High-quality, lightweight camping equipment. Great service and guarantee. Write: 110 Prefontaine Pl, Seattle, WA 98104.

Marmot Mountain Works: Expensive sleeping bags, but I've had one for ten years. Excellent quality. Guarantee. Catalog. Write: 331 S. 13th St., Grand Junction, CO 81501.

L.L. Bean: One of the best. Sleeping bags, bikes, tents, all your equipment needs. Excellent guarantee. Catalog. Write: Casco St., Freeport, ME 04033. Call: 1-800-341-4341.

Army/Navy Surplus Stores: You can find one in any large city. The stores carry quality gear at budget prices. Look in your local phone book for "Army/Navy Store."

Bicycle Organizations

American Youth Hostels: If you're on a long-distance tour, you'll find that YHAs are located in 5,500 places around the globe. With your YHA card, you can spend the night for a minimum charge. You may enjoy a hot shower, bed, cooking area, books and great ambiance. You'll meet many world travelers. You need a hostel bed sheet to use the bunks. Write: YHA, Metro Council, 132 Spring Street, New York 10012.

Bicycle Institute Of America: Directory of bicycle clubs in America. Write: 122 E. 42nd St., New York, NY 10017.

League Of American Wheelman: For women, too. This organization can help you with touring, commuting and racing activities. Write: 19 S. Bothwell, Palatine, IL 60067.

Bikecentennial: For touring trans-America. Trail guides, tour maps and routes, newsletter, group tours. Write: P.O. Box 8308, Missoula, MT 59807.

Magazines About Bicycling And Touring

Bicycling and *Mountain Bike*: Covers all of bicycling. Not much on touring. Writes on latest designs and trends. Will help you find touring companies in the states and abroad. The last article I wrote for this magazine was titled: "The Ugliest Man In Montana." Write: 33 E. Minor St., Emmaus, PA 18049.

Adventure Cyclist: This magazine, published nine times a year, is devoted exclusively to touring. Write: Adventure Cyclist, P.O. Box 8308, Missoula, MT 59807.

Campground Sources

Rand McNally offers *Campground and Trailer Park Guide,* as well as booklets about campgrounds in every section of the United States.

National Touring Companies

You may be looking for a specific type of touring experience within the United States of America. No matter if you're new or experienced, you can find any kind of style of tour that fits you. Different tours feature a multitude of approaches, from guided to self-contained, roughing it to sag wagon-supported with all meals and beds prepared for you. You can ride on a budget or you can tour like Prince Charles (Lady Diana not included). If money is no object, you can ride in a rickshaw – but you'll have to tip the poor devil who has to pedal you up that 10,000 foot mountain pass.

American Wilderness Experience - All Adventure Travel: If you're in a hurry, and want to set up a guided tour, you're in good hands with this company. They offer a 48-page color brochure with one thousand bike tours from top operators around the world. They will set you up in any style you prefer. You can customize your tour by booking into backpacking treks or river raft adventures. Call: 1-800-444-0099.

Back Country: First-class, inn-to-inn biking adventure vacation packages. Offers a guarantee. Bike the West, Alaska, New Zealand, Hawaii. Rent bikes in three styles – tandem, mountain, full suspension. Limited group size. Ask for brochure. Write: P.O. Box 4029, Bozeman, MT, 59722. Call: 1-800-575-1540.

Backroads: Quality tours and cuisine, for all abilities and levels, ages. Catalog. Call: 1-800-462-2848.

Adventure Bicycling: For more serious cyclists. Focus on western states. Sag wagon supported. Cycle in Alaska, Canadian Rockies, Oregon coast, Cascades, Puget Sound, Bryce, Zion, Grand Canyon, New Mexico, California. Brochure. Write: Timberline, 7975 E. Harvard #J, Denver, CO. Call: 1-800-417-2453.

Around The World Odyssey 2000: Bicyclists who are completely out of their minds will love this adventure! I rode with this company on a West Coast trek in 1995. Sag wagon support. The company offers a 20,000-mile, 54-country, around-the-world tour from January 1 through December 31, 2000. The group also offers cross-country treks at all levels. Write: Tim Kneeland, 200 Lake Washington Blvd., Suite 101, Seattle, WA 98122. Call: 1-800-433-0528.

Bike Vermont: This is a smaller, friendlier inn-to-inn touring company. All levels. Support van. Tour leaders. Twentieth year. Write: Box 207M, Woodstock, VT 05091. Call: 1-800-257-2226. Some of you old baby boomers might like to go back to Woodstock to feel young again. You could sniff the air for remains of your youth. Good luck.

International Touring Companies

Before you take off on a self-contained tour, you may want to get your feet wet by going on a guided tour. Once you feel confident, the world is your home.

CBT Bicycle Tours: One- to seven-day tours. All levels. Support van. Hotels, bed and breakfast inns, campgrounds. Write: 415 W. Fullerton, #1003, Chicago, IL 60614. Call: 1-800-736-2453.

Euro-Bike Tours: In business 23 years. Luxury European tours. Tour 15 countries. All levels. Brochure. Write: P.O. Box 990-U, DeKalb, IL 60115. Call: 1-800-321-6060.

Australian Adventures: Top-quality touring company. Thirteen individual tours and leaders. Will map out self-guided tours for you. Write: Peregrine Adventures, 12115 100th Ave. NE, Kirkland, WA 98034. Call: 1-800-889-1464.

Van Gogh Bicycle Tours: Bicycle Holland, Austria, France. Bike and barge vacation tours. Guides. Small groups. Catered. All levels. Call: 1-800-488-8332.

Easy Ride Tours: Bicycle Portugal, Spain, Azores, Ireland, Nova Scotia, Prince Edward Island. Exceptional cuisine. All levels. Fascinating routes. Call: 1-800-488-8332.

New Zealand Pedal Tours: Local guides, Inns, quiet roads, incredible scenery. Tenth year. North and South Islands. Write: Down Under Answers, 1611 Market Street, Kirkland, WA 98033. Call: 1-800-788-6685.

Bicyclists Looking For Riding Partners

You may be planning a bicycle tour around the world. Perhaps you're taking a summer trip across America. You don't want to go alone and you don't know anyone who will go with you.

The easiest thing for you to do is check *Outside* magazine's "Outside Mart" for people placing want ads for partners. If you can't find any that fit your plans, place your own ad. Be specific. You may meet a friend for life. Always take time to get to know another person before going on a tour together. Bike touring is like being married to that person 24 hours per day. If you have any doubts about getting along, you need to figure that out before leaving on the trip.

A bicycle tour can turn into a nightmare if you're with the wrong person. Think things out before hand. Do you want a male or female companion? Experienced or inexperienced cyclist? Languages? Educational background? Introvert or extrovert? Length of trip? Miles you plan on making per day? Age? Places to travel? Months on the road? When are you going?

To place an ad, write to: *Outside* magazine, in care of "The Outside Mart" editor, 400 Market St., Santa Fe, NM 87501.

Glossary

Allen key/wrench: A small L-shaped wrench that fits inside the head of a bolt or screw.

Baby boomer: Person riding a bicycle who refuses to get old even though they're balding and using Prozac to alter their personality and be more like their kids. They have lots of money, but no time. Bicycle touring could save their lives.

Bottom bracket: The cylindrical part of a bicycle frame that holds the crank axle.

Brake pad: A block of rubber-like material fastened to the end of a brake caliper. It presses against the wheel rim when the brakes are applied.

Braze-ons: Parts for mounting shift levers, derailleurs, bottle cages and racks. The braze-ons are fastened to the bike frame through a soldering process known as brazing.

Bungee Cords: Stretch cords covered with cloth that have two hooks on the ends. Used to secure gear to racks on bicycle.

Cage: This is found on a front derailleur. It's a pair of parallel plates that push the chain from side to side to shift it back and forth among three chainrings.

Caliper: These are brake arms that reach around the sides of a wheel to press brake pads against the wheel rim.

Candle lantern: A small candle encased in a metal/glass jacket that can be used for reading, cooking or lighting the way to the showers. It's also used for romantic interludes.

Chain: Linked metal "rope" that connects the chain wheel to the back wheel.

Chain ring: Metal sprocket attached to the right crank arm to drive the chain.

Chainstays: The two tubes of a bicycle frame that run from the bottom bracket back to the rear dropouts.

Crank arm: A part, one end of which is attached to the bottom bracket axle and the other to a pedal, whose forward rotation provides the leverage needed to power the bicycle.

Crankset: A group of components that includes the bottom bracket,two crankarms and one or more chainrings.

Derailleur: A lever-activated mechanism that pushes the chain off of one sprocket and onto another, thus changing the gear ratio.

Dish: This is the offset of the hub in a rear wheel on a derailleur to make room for the freewheel and still allow the wheel to be centered within the frame.

Down tube: The tube running from the headset to the bottom bracket. One part of the main triangle on a bicycle frame.

Drive train: The derailleurs, chain, freewheel and crankset of the bike.

Dropout: A slot in the frame into which the rad wheel axle fits.

Dropout hanger: A threaded metal piece that extends below the right rear dropout, used as a mount for the rear derailleur.

Drops: The lower, straight portion of a turned-down-type handlebar set.

Established campground: A campground with toilets, water, picnic tables, possibly showers, trash receptacles. Usually costs money.

Flange: The parts of a hub shell to which spokes are attached.

Fork: The part of the frame that fits inside the head tube and holds the front wheel.

Fork blades: The parallel curved tubes that hold the front wheel.

Freewheel: A removable component attached to the rear hub on most bikes. It carries gear cogs on the outside and contains a ratcheting mechanism inside that allows the wheel to rotate forward while the pedals, chain and gear sprockets remain still or move in reverse.

Granny: Slang term for the tiny innermost chain ring on a triple chain ring crankset. It is the lowest gear possible and used for steep or long climbs.

Gloves: Padded gloves with open fingers to protect palms and ulnar nerve from too much pressure.

Handlebar bag: A compartment attached to the handlebars for holding food, camera, sunblock, knife, wallet, etc.

Headset: The combination of cups, cones and ball bearings that creates the bearing mechanism that allows the fork column to rotate inside the head tube.

Head Tube: The shortest tube in the main triangle. The front forks are housed inside the head tube.

Helmet: Used by smart bicyclists to protect their heads in case of a fall. Helmet is strapped to the head around the jaw by a nylon strap and clip.

High Five: When two cyclists have grunted and groaned their way to the top of a 12,000-foot pass, they raise their hands in triumph and smack each other's palms in jubilation. "Oh what a feeling, Toyota!"

Hub: The center of a wheel where the spokes attach. It contains an axle with two sets of bearings, bearing cones, washers, lock nuts and parts for attaching the wheel to the frame.

Index shifters: Shifting levers that click into distinct positions that correspond to certain freewheel cogs and don't require fine-tuning after each shift.

Knobby tires: Heavy tires with large knobs to provide traction in wet, muddy terrain. Not good for touring.

Lug: An external metal sleeve that holds two or more tubes together at the joints of a frame.

Macho: A little butterfly from the rain forests in Brazil that has a peanut-shaped fuselage. Its bite creates a desperate sexual need that must be satisfied within 24 hours or the person may die. Reports are inconclusive as to the veracity of this fairy tale.

Master link: A special link on a bicycle chain that can be opened by flexing a plate, removing a screw, or by some means other than driving out a rivet.

Miner's lamp: A battery-powered lamp attached around the head by flexible cloth bands and used to cook food or light the way to the rest room without running into a tree branch.

Mountain bike/All-terrain bike: A bicycle with fat tires, straight handle-bars and a wide range of gearing designed for offroad use.

Nipple: A small metal piece that fits through a wheel rim and is threaded inside to receive the end of the spoke.

Panniers: For touring, four large bags that hold a touring cyclist's possessions. They attach to front and rear racks and look like modern day saddlebags.

Presta valve: A bicycle tube valve whose stem has a small nut on top.

Primitive campsite: A campsite located in the wilds with no human conveniences. You're right out there with the bears and bees.

Quick release: A cam-lever mechanism used to rapidly tighten or loosen a wheel on a bike frame, seat post, or brake cable within a cable housing.

Rain gear: Special jacket/with hood, and pants, along with shoe protection that touring cyclists wear to keep protected.

Rim: A metal wheel that holds the tire, tube and the outer ends of the spokes.

Rear view mirror: A mirror mounted on a cyclist's eyeglasses, helmet or handlebars that allows vision to the rear. It's nice to be able to see if a drunk is going to run you over so you can jump off the bike to save yourself.

Saddle: Seat on a bicycle.

Schrader valve: A tire valve similar to the type on auto tires.

Seat post: The part to which the saddle clamps and which runs down the inside of the seat tube.

Sore butt: A condition brought about by sitting to many hours on a bike seat without raising off while coasting down hill, or by not stopping to rest often.

Spanner: Same as a wrench. Aussie or English origins.

Spider: The multi-armed piece to which the chain wheels are bolted, usually welded to or part of the right crank arm.

Spoke: One of the several wires used to hold hub in the center of a wheel rim and to transfer the load from the perimeter of the wheel to the hub and on to the frame.

Sprocket: A disk bearing teeth for driving a chain.

Stuff sack: A nylon sack with a purse-string closure that holds large items like sleeping bags and small items like cook stoves or utensils.

Tandem: A bicycle built for two!

Alligator tears: These happen when you're cutting up an onion for your gourmet dinner. Also, these tears could fall if you forget your bicycle pump and you suffer a flat tire in the middle of the Sahara Desert.

Tights: Lycra or wool clothing worn over legs to protect from cold or severe sunlight.

Ulnar Nerve: A nerve in the hand that makes the hand go numb if a rider doesn't have properly padded riding gloves or doesn't lift his or her hands off the bars and shake them out often.

Wheel base: The distance between the front and the rear axles on a bicycle.

X-Generation: A group of Americans who have no purpose and can't find meaning in their lives. They seem to be lost in America. A simple cure might be a bicycle tour.